Classical Indiscretions

Classical Indiscretions

A millennial enquiry into the state of the Classics

Maurizio Bettini

translated by
John McManamon

edited by
Rebecca Langlands

Duckworth

First published in English in 2001 by
Gerald Duckworth & Co. Ltd.
61 Frith Street
London W1D 3JL
Tel: 020 7434 4242
Fax: 020 7434 4420
Email: inquiries@duckworth-publishers.co.uk
www.ducknet.co.uk

Original Italian title *I classici nell' età dell' indiscrezione*
© 1995 Giulio Einaudi editore s.p.a. Torino, Italy

English translation © 2001 by John McManamon

A catalogue record for this book is available
from the British Library

ISBN 0 7156 2970 0

Typeset by Derek Doyle & Associates, Liverpool
Printed in Great Britain by
Biddles Ltd, *www.biddles.co.uk*

Contents

To my friend Beniamino Placido,
who taught me that the spirit of
the classics blows *ubi vult*.

Preface

Almost everything about the Greek and Latin classics is up for debate, other than their antiquity: we measure their existence on a scale of millennia. It follows that they reflect cultural worlds very different from our own: difficult worlds, which at times allow entry only to those armed with a good commentary; archaic worlds, so far removed from our own that they often seem unreal.

On the other hand, the classics existed when almost all Western literature had yet to be written, and they thus constitute what we have in common with the generations that preceded us. It's important to have some books in common with others. For example, if you discover that you and your neighbour both own a copy of Lampedusa's famous novel, *The Leopard*, this knowledge may somehow alleviate the problems of living in the same block of flats. Or you might learn through the family grapevine that 'Your grandfather also had a lively interest in Stevenson.' But what books can we imagine having in common with, say, Dante? Not Stevenson's, but certainly Vergil's. We share Vergil with Dante, with St Augustine, and with the emperor Augustus. The classics comprise our 'common language' – shared not only with the past but with all who come from that past.

The fact is that even if we had been born at almost any other time in our recorded history, we would still find the classics, in very much the same form, in existence. They were around when Christians began to persecute pagans (for the very reason that the pagans insisted on their right to read the classics); but they were also around before that, when pagans began to persecute Christians. To pinpoint a precise moment: when Christ set out on the roads of Galilee, a significant proportion of the classics as we know them had already been around for some time, and were circulating in editions with commentaries, very much like our own.

The classics have been studied for over two thousand years, and during that time they have been read in the most diverse circumstances and disparate places. To confine ourselves to a few examples, let's begin by imagining the library at Alexandria, established in the third century before Christ, where Zenodotus is annotating papyrus scrolls on which the poems of Homer are written; then let's move to Rome and sit next to Crates of Mallos, the ambassador who broke his leg and, unable to leave his couch, passed the time by giving the Romans their first lessons in philology. (Thus philology took root in Rome because an ambassador from Attalus of Pergamum tripped over a sewer cover.) As we continue on our journey, we reach the library of Augustus, pass on rapidly through the court of the Carolingian emperors to the monasteries of the early middle ages, vault briefly into the schools of the Jesuits, and file into the ageing lecture halls of the twenty-first century. Everywhere we find ourselves face to face with the classics, and everywhere they are very much the same.

Today we can read the classics on the underground, in a plane, or in front of the television. Caesar and Plato regularly commute between Rome and Tokyo; Vergil is quite at home in the era of the chat-show. As one might expect, all this has had consequences for our way of looking at the classics, but I don't think it bothers *them* in the least. On the contrary, we might even expect some help from the classics as we try to understand what is going on around us today. They have witnessed a great deal, and who knows how much more they have yet to see?

1

The Age of Futility

Haec sciam? Et quid ignorem?
(Do I need to know these things? And what can I afford to ignore?)

These questions were posed by the Roman philosopher Seneca in one of his letters to Lucilius:[1] with his customary rhetorical skill he had them cap a long list of erudite trivia. The issue was this: the grammarian Didymus had written four thousand volumes in which he discussed questions such as who Aeneas' mother really was, whether the lyric poet Anacreon was more of a lech than a lush, whether the poetess Sappho was a prostitute, and how Hecuba could be the same age as Helen and yet have aged with so little grace, and so on. Seneca felt that it was not deciding *whether* it was necessary to know things of this sort that was the problem, but rather that once one had decided that it *was* important to know whether Anacreon was more of a lech than a lush, then there was no longer anything that it was possible to ignore.

Seneca scorned those who wasted their time on useless literary problems (*qui litterarum inutilium studiis detinentur*). In another of his works, *On the Shortness of Life*, he raised the stakes:

It used to be a Greek disease, investigating how many rowers Odysseus had, whether the *Iliad* or the *Odyssey* was written first, whether they are even by the same author, and other matters of this kind, which, if you keep them to yourself, do you no good, and, if you publish them, just make you look boring. But now this vain passion for learning useless things (*inane studium supervacua discendi*) has assailed the Romans as well. A few days ago I heard someone explaining what it was that each Roman general was the first to do: Duilius was the first to win a naval battle; Curius Dentatus was the first to lead elephants in a triumph. ... We can forgive someone who tries to discover the name of the person who first induced the Romans to board a ship: it was Claudius, nicknamed Caudex. ... We may also see some merit in the information that Valerius Corvinus was the first to conquer Messana. ... But must I also be interested in the fact that Lucius Sulla was the first to exhibit lions at loose in the circus ... and that javelin-throwers were sent by King Bocchus to finish them off?[2]

Why indeed should we care if King Bocchus sent some javelin-throwers to kill Sulla's lions? It is ridiculous to waste precious time on such matters, time which could be spent learning about, or even just thinking about, more important things. And of course Seneca did not foresee the invention of the mass media. He lived in an era in which a supreme example of triviality was the need to know the exact number of rowers used by Odysseus. It was not yet a question of knowing the details of the erotic phone calls made by Prince Charles to his friend Camilla, or the exact number of pandas left in the Himalayas. The *inane studium supervacua discendi* has once again descended upon us, but this time it has assumed the proportions of a great flood. An interviewer addresses a professor of psychology on television: 'In a few hours you will enter the cell of a serial killer. What questions will you put to him?' *Haec sciam? et quid ignorem?*

Sooner or later, for practical reasons, we must face the problem of how to set some kind of limit on the information we can absorb. Not as a form of moral censorship, because we feel it would be better if some people were kept ignorant of certain matters, but simply because there are certain things that are absolutely not worth knowing. In the same letter to

1. The Age of Futility

Lucilius, Seneca added 'Have pity on time!' (*tempori parce*). We do not generally think of time as a living creature that can feel pain, yet every day time suffers an incredible amount of informational torture. In the normal course of events, we tend to behave as follows: we assume that anything we *can* know is worth knowing. And since the mass media offer us, at least in theory, the possibility of knowing everything, we feel it is right to be totally informed. We have been caught off guard by the media explosion, and we no longer know how to do without. We are just like people who have been poor for centuries and suddenly find themselves immersed in consumer society: faced with the dubious delights of the supermarket they cannot contain themselves but just go on getting fatter and fatter.

We need an information diet book. We are buried under the latest news, amazing scoops, exclusive reports – unequal in value and importance, but all meant for simultaneous consumption in vast quantities:

> An actress has had her breast and lips reconstructed ... In Bosnia twelve children have been found murdered in a school ... A former government minister is accused of having Mafia connections ... The motorway is closed to traffic at Junction 5 (*thank goodness I had the radio on*) ...

It all gets lumped together:

> Beep, beep: the time is now 10 o'clock ... Here's why Vivaldi published his first sheet music in Holland and not in Venice ... Will Paola of Liège, the 'belle Italienne' who has now become queen, succeed in winning the trust of the Belgian people?

It all seems a huge muddle, and it is. But close observation suggests that there is a certain order to the whole. An arcane and unruly order, granted, yet it *does* exist. In essence, it

11

consists of the same order that governs the thought processes of magic, namely the conviction that things relate to one another not on the basis of logical or practical connections, but through the workings of a secret *sympatheia*, according to which links are established – usually unexpected links between entities that are quite incompatible. Indeed, for the magical process to be set in motion, it is enough for two objects to 'resemble' each other or to have had some kind of 'contact'. Thus, in order to win back a lost lover, the magician sprinkles potions over an image of the unfaithful partner or does things with a lock of hair from the deserted partner. In both cases – an image that resembles the beloved, or a lock of hair that has come into contact with her body – a *sympatheia* will be established. But the *sympatheia* is a demon. And the way it behaves, even when it is used to organise the everyday expression of our culture, does not contradict its basic nature.

It is the *sympatheia* that ruthlessly gathers images and patterns, making use of extremely remote 'contacts' and of 'resemblances' that are often purely arbitrary. Seneca's problem is becoming increasingly urgent: if we must know all these things, what can we ever choose *not* to know? The world seems extraordinarily complex. It is full of stuff – monuments, wells, cars, parrots ... – as well as being populated by billions of people. Anything can be turned into a subject of discussion or, more precisely, into a news bulletin. The mine is truly inexhaustible – just thinking about the tiniest part of it makes you dizzy. It reminds me of Borges' character, Carlos Argentino Daneri, who decided to devote his life to an exhaustive description of all the places on earth – in effect, to describe the whole world.[3] By 1941 he had managed to cover several hectares in the state of Queensland as well as a gasometer in the region of Vera Cruz. But that still left him with a lot of things to describe! And there is no doubt that his ambitious poem (we could call it *Descriptio totius orbis locu-*

pletissima) was fated to remain unfinished. Nevertheless, to transform the world into a subject for discussion is an undertaking at once simple and limitless. You only have to find an excuse for speaking on any given subject, and the game is on. The information has been generated.

Carlos Argentino Daneri had a mythological predecessor worth mentioning here. I mean Sisyphus, the hero who was condemned to an eternity of rolling a large boulder up a hill. He could never reach the top, for the boulder would roll down the hill when he was just short of the summit, and he would have to start all over again. Sisyphus is the true hero of our age – lord and master of any activity associated with the media. We are all condemned, as producers and consumers of information, to expend an enormous amount of energy in pushing large boulders up hills. Indeed, a Japanese scholar recently proposed a new interpretation of the myth. Instead of seeing Sisyphus as exemplifying the futility and vanity of all human action, he regards him as a moral hero. For to perform pointless actions, which you know from the start are doomed to remain unfinished, exalts the pure content of human activity, without purpose and therefore absolutely moral. This interpretation certainly seems to some extent inspired by the models of behaviour that dominate the assembly lines of the Toyota Corporation. But is it not interesting that a Japanese scholar, living at the heart of the purest technological modernity, recognises himself not in Odysseus or Herakles, but in Sisyphus?

2

The Tyranny of Time

The era of the calendar

As if the surface of the earth and the vast number of its inhabitants were not enough to generate culture, we also have the calendar at our disposal. Since the classics often find themselves closely involved in a process that we might describe as 'compiling a cultural calendar', we had better treat the subject in some detail.

In any year there are 365 days available for use. And, given that our civilisation – even at a conservative estimate – is at least 2,500 years old, the cultural calendar has 365 x 2,500 opportunities to exploit. In what sense? Well, that should be obvious. In the sense that the calendar of one year, projected back over the years of our illustrious history, allows us in theory to identify at least 912,500 people who were born or who died on the same day as 'today' across the span of the 2,500 years already behind us. This gives us an excuse to transmit a brief biography, or excerpts from their works, or perhaps even a picture.

Let us say that 'today' is 15 August. On 15 August 1797 a certain Arthur Radcliffe-Brown, author of that fundamental work of astrophysics, *Speculum deiectionis* (*Mirror of Dejection*) was born; on the same day in 994, some Saxons who were still pagans martyred St Cinivulfa. Nor is it only a question of births and deaths. We also have to take into account battles, declarations of independence, train wrecks and plane crashes, decisions that transformed the face of our

14

world. One can feel the excitement of generating this information from the 912,500 possibilities offered by the calendar!
And that is without taking into account that the same day
may generate more than one event – multiple births and
deaths, for example. It makes one's head spin. The global
numbers of historic events per day – by which I mean the
treasure held by almanacs and cultural calendars – is truly
enormous.

The use of the calendar to generate cultural opportunities
functions by means of a mechanism that linguists call a
'shifter', which means roughly 'something that moves' or
'something that slides'. Take the expression 'today'. Clearly it
is a temporal definition, but it doesn't have a fixed character:
it is a definition that shifts. You can say 'today' just as accu-
rately for 14 April 2000 as for 3 July 1791, provided that you
are using the word to refer to the same day on which you
utter it. The suggestive powers of this shifting mechanism are
immediately apparent. If I say on TV, '210 years ago today,
such and such happened', I compel viewers to assume a
perspective squarely positioned in the eighteenth century.
Once they have done this, I can broadcast images of people in
powdered wigs to the accompaniment of Haydn's *Surprise
Symphony*. And I can adjust things to fit the period, fashion
or music of any time and place.

The apotheosis of ten

In our culture, ever in search of excuses to supply more information, the calendar has assumed a wholly unprecedented
importance. That is all the more true because we not only
have 'today', but also 'this year', another shifter that functions in exactly the same way but with even greater potential
for violence. The expression 'this year' can shift back as far as
you like, but in this case the shifting is considered valid on

condition that it produce a round number: fifty years ago ...,
a hundred years ago ..., two hundred years ago.... It is not
permissible to shift back by a figure such as, let's say, forty-
six years. Poliomyelitis is a terrible disease, and the vaccine
discovered by Sabin undoubtedly constitutes one of the most
beneficial and significant achievements of medical research.
Unfortunately, however, it was discovered only forty-six years
ago so we are not in a position to consider the discovery
important. We have even less cause to mention it. We have to
wait four more years and round the number up to fifty.

This limitation is not fortuitous, nor is it the result of some
arbitrary convention. At the base of our predilection for
'round numbers' lies one of the most solid foundations of our
tradition, the adoption of a decimal system as a means of
calculation. When we count, as everyone knows, we take as
our base the number ten. Once we have used up the first ten
numbers, each of which has its own name, we continue by
adding these very same numbers to the number ten, after
which we move on, multiplying the number ten further and
further to reach the higher levels. The very structure of our
counting system highlights the number ten and its multiples.

But numbers are not just used for counting; they also function as symbolic agents, at least according to the discipline
known as numerology. Numerology is cherished by magi-
cians, occultists, investigators of lost civilisations, and so on,
but fortunately it is also cultivated by anthropologists and
folklorists. If the number three symbolises completeness or
perfection, the number seven and its multiples, at least as
used in the Bible, serve to communicate the significance of
'the innumerable'. Folklore has always made use of the
number twelve to indicate 'companions who belong to the
same group',[1] for example the twelve apostles. In the area of
temporal shifting the number ten has assumed the same
mythical and symbolic importance as the numbers three,

seven or twelve possess in other areas of our cultural tradition. When you start counting years, the number ten, and to
an even greater extent its multiples, immediately announce:
'There's an anniversary to celebrate!'

This temporal shifting by round numbers, or calendrical
apotheosis of the number ten, corresponds to what we call an
anniversary, or more usually a centennial, a bicentennial, a
quincentennial, and so on. Our civilisation is quite old, so the
anniversary game is not only extremely easy to play but very
powerful: the number of events you can reach by subtracting
a multiple of ten from the year we are now in is almost
infinite.

However, to play the anniversary game you need a proper
board, a bit like the board for Snakes and Ladders. This is
something anyone can make at home, though its construction
requires a bit of time and effort. Let me give a brief description for the intelligent reader.

The anniversary board

In order to get started you'll need to lay your hands on a very
large piece of vertically lined paper. For now, leave the
heading of the first column on the left blank; at the top of
each of the remaining columns, insert the following labels:
'writers', 'poets', 'statesmen', 'scientists', 'scientific discoveries', 'declarations of war', 'proclamations of magnae
cartae', 'eruptions of volcanoes', 'battles that changed the
course of history', and so on. Now, at the top of the first
column on the left, insert the rubric 'chronology'. Since you
are in this column, the trickiest one of all, continue to work
on it, carrying out the following operation with the utmost
care: proceeding strictly from top to bottom, write down in
order every year of our history – and I mean every single one
– from the eighth century before Christ[2] to the present. Next,

under each year, trace a horizontal line, cutting across all the vertical columns, so that you end up with a series of small blocks in a row. Once you have completed this phase of the operation, you will have a board that resembles an enormous crossword puzzle without any black squares – the sort that only the experts manage to solve.

The second phase of the operation requires extreme care, and you should only carry it out with the assistance of authoritative encyclopaedias or approved textbooks. It consists of carefully inserting in each small square of each column ('writers', 'poets', 'statesmen', etc.) persons or events according to the corresponding year of their birth, or their death, or their occurrence. Next to each person or event, be sure to insert a precise definition of the place where the person was born or died, or the event took place. This operation will prove of fundamental importance when you pass on to the phase of implementation, by which I mean the phone survey.

But let's not get ahead of ourselves. First, let me give you an example of what you'll find in front of you once you've filled in the individual squares of the respective columns by proceeding as instructed. In 63 BC Octavian, the individual who will later be called Augustus, was born (category: 'persons who have changed the course of history'); Cicero was elected consul (category: 'events that have changed the course of history'), while Catullus, a young man of great promise from the Po Valley, moved to Rome (category: 'poets'). As for the category 'wars and battles', it was in that same year that Pompey victoriously concluded his campaign against Mithridates. There you are. You now have at your disposal an instrument of incredible power and duration. You need only use it intelligently and keep close at hand a sufficient stack of this strips of paper, which I like to call 'the anniversary strips' or 'the shifter facilitators'.

18

2. *The Tyranny of Time*

You need to collect a substantial bunch of these strips, of variable width and of sufficient length to cover the entire vertical extension of the board. Pick one of them up and cut it to a fifty-year length, then take a second and cut it to a hundred years, and so on, increasing the length by round numbers until you reach the date furthest from you and nearest to 800 BC . Once you have finished the cutting operation, lay each individual strip in turn against the 'chronology' column and mark with a cross the individual years you have singled out in this way. If you start in 2001, the strip 'fifty years ago' will automatically take you to 1951, that for 'one hundred years ago'; to 1901, that for 'one thousand years ago' to 1001, and so forth. Now take a wooden or plastic ruler and, by each cross that you have pencilled in, trace a horizontal line in red so that it cuts across each column ('writers', 'poets', 'statesmen', 'scientists', 'scientific discoveries', 'battles', etc.). This is an exciting moment. If you've done things properly, you will have before you a complete table – relating to the current year – of all the possible anniversaries, in almost every field of human history and knowledge, across a span of almost 3,000 years. Isn't it amazing? Examine it column by column. Which anniversaries do you have at your disposal under the heading 'poets'? *Voilà*: the centennial of the birth of Angioino Tetrastilo, one hundred and fifty years after the death of Svevo Biturini. And in the field of scientific discoveries? Exactly three hundred years ago, the subcephalic membranes of giant lepids were finally given a name and a description, one hundred and fifty years ago the spores of *gadgetistris* revealed the secret of their immunity to chamomile.

Do not make the mistake of discarding the strips! Next year, you will have to add the current year to the bottom of the 'chronology' column, and then repeat the procedure of marking the pencilled crosses and drawing in the red lines.

19

The board is a lasting acquisition, but the shifter which gives form to the anniversary obviously requires annual updating.

At this point I can reveal that the anniversary board has a name. It is a *Conspectus festorum anniversariorum per sigla quadrata* (Tabulated overview of anniversary celebrations) and will be known from now on by that solemn Latin nomenclature. To all of you who have drawn one, I suggest that you now acquire a good telephone directory. You should get one with the numbers of all the mayors and heads of local councils of all decent-sized towns and cities, and of the relevant spokespeople for the local arts organisations, and above all of the chief executives of banks and the general administrators of important government offices. Why? Because a good telephone directory is essential if you are to pass on to the phase of implementation – when you reap the benefits of all your hard work on the table.

Manufacturing a centennial

Once you are seated comfortably in your favourite chair, surrounded by your *Conspectus festorum anniversariorum per sigla quadrata*, which by now will have assumed the dimensions of your dining room floor, you can relax and call – let's see – the mayor of the municipality in which Angioino Tetrastilo was born. Ask him this simple question: 'Mayor, are you aware that this year marks the centennial of the birth of Angioino Tetrastilo, renowned poet of your town of Somma Campanula?' The mayor will tell you that he was not aware of it and does not have a clue who the devil Angioino Tetrastilo is: 'I've never even heard the name – I've only been mayor for a few months.' Now don't panic. After you have talked to him for a few minutes you will be pleasantly surprised to find yourself taken very seriously. Once the mayor has got over his initial defensiveness, he will admit that he really likes the idea of celebrating the centennial of the birth of Angioino Tetrastilo. 'Somma Campanula,' he will say, 'needs to set aside a moment for study and reflection, a sublime moment.'

And all this excitement for the centennial of Tetrastilo who was, without wishing to cause offence, a rather mediocre poet. On one occasion, enraptured by the beauty of Somma Campanula, he praised his home town thus:

> The peace that I experience
> In the heart, and the joyful
> Pealing from your
> Churches, and the groups of tourists
> Are lifting me to God.

A rare example of the mysticism of tourism. However, Tetrastilo's reputation will surely be enhanced when he is commemorated one afternoon in the Town Hall, if only because he took tourism seriously. There will also be the live testimony of his cousin Gaspar, who accompanied the poet on his famous trip to Spain. There they attended a bullfight. Take a look at his poem, Bullfighter, inspired by that experience:

> In the arena the bull fights,
> In the arena the bull gets run through.
> Blood and bull and bullfighter
> In the arena ...

In the case of Tetrastilo we are dealing with little more than the crumbs of celebration – to be blunt, with rank provincialism. But we have seen what happened in Paris and all over Europe for the bicentennial of the French Revolution: a veritable plethora of initiatives. To say nothing of the five hundredth anniversary of the so-called 'discovery' of America which generated not only celebrations and conferences but also building projects of startling dimensions. In the modern world the power of the calendar intimidates cities and makes them do whatever it wants. It demands budgets, appropriations, kickbacks.

The bimillennium and the universal holocaust

If the calendar truly exercises such power, what were we to expect in 2000, when we marked not only the bimillennium of the birth of Christ but the anniversary of anniversaries, the autoanniversary of the calendar? For the bimillennium of the birth of Christ coincides with the bimillennium of that fateful day from which we calculate the celebration of all other anniversiaries – a sort of 'birthday of all birthdays' (*dies natalis omnium natalium dierum*). Go and sit down for a second in the middle of your *Conspectus festorum anniversariorum per sigla quadrata*. You will find that everything – every single thing – begins from the year zero, the mystical point at which BC and AD meet. In all likelihood, you will find the birth of Christ directly under your chair.

We have just experienced the great Jubilee of the year 2000. We have seen with our own eyes the incredible convulsion caused by a mere accident of the calendar. Rome taken over first by all sorts of road works, then by the invasion of millions of pilgrims; the Pope on television every evening, celebrating the Children's Jubilee, the Farmers' Jubilee, the Carpenters' Jubilee, the Intellectuals' Jubilee, and so on. A storm of Catholic and Christian culture broke over our heads, promoted by books, TV debates and speeches by bishops and intellectuals. And this was still nothing compared with the Church's decision, on the occasion of the Jubilee, to reveal to the world the so-called 'third mystery of Fatima', in other words the last of the three visions of the Madonna experienced by Portuguese shepherd children in long-ago 1917, and a jealously-guarded secret up to now. Thus we learned that in their third encounter with the Madonna the shepherds saw a bishop dressed in white falling under a hail of gunfire by dangerous natives. A very naïve story, and above all very general, as any prophetic vision must be. Yet even this 'revelation' sparked off an incredible number of comments, arguments and analyses, in newspapers that up to then had been regarded as serious, and by intellectuals who, up to then, were above all suspicion. So has Italy returned to being an overwhelmingly Catholic country, simply because of an accident of dates?

How great are the virtues of the calendar, one might exclaim. If only it were true. But I don't believe it will last. The cult of the anniversary is as generous as it is ruthless: and the rule goes, 'As soon as we've enjoyed one anniversary, let's find another to celebrate.' Otherwise, what are newspapers and TV to talk about? I don't believe that the 2000th anniversary of the birth of Christ can escape this rule; even such a momentous event must succumb to the consequences of its entry into the calendar game, that is to say: oblivion. The age of the calendar is rigid. The same factors that lavish success, a high-profile image, visibility (as communication experts tell us) also result in oblivion for the event that has had its day.

Still, coincidences can prove unnerving. The Stoic philosophers, for example, attributed great significance to such conjunctions – they felt that the very existence of the cosmos depended on them. 'The Stoics,' Nemesius claimed, 'assert that when the planets are once again arranged in the same constellations, at the same height and position as they were at the beginning, when the cosmos first came into being, they will bring about the conflagration and destruction of all things.'[3] this is the theory of the universal holocaust (*ekpyrhosis*), which will consume the entire cosmos at the end of the 'great year' when each part of the cosmos, through its own unceasing motion, reaches the identical position that it occupied at the moment of creation. The Stoics also held that, once the fatal holocaust had burned itself out, the world would be reborn, or more precisely restarted exactly as it was, with the same conditions and the same people. Nemesius went on:

> Then, starting anew from the beginning, the world is established exactly as it was before, and the stars go through their motions all over again; each one of them, just as they did in the previous world-cycle, will go back to completing its course through the heavens without variation. And there will be a new Socrates and a new Plato, and each will be the same and have the same friends and the same fellow Athenian citizens ... and every city, village and division of the countryside will likewise be repeated.

A passage from Tatian is even more explicit: 'Zeno reveals that after the holocaust the same men rise again to behave exactly as before – I mean Anytus and Meletus[4] to prosecute, Busiris to kill his guests, and Herakles to labour over again.'[5] There does not seem to be much hope for the world: once the *ekpyrhosis* has burned out, there will be other informers, other murderers, other heroes. But they will not be 'others', they will be exactly the same ones.

So the Stoics imagined that once the 'great year' had ended and the cosmic holocaust had burned itself out, a second world would be set in motion – an exact copy of the first, inhabited by doubles of all those who had lived previously with exactly the same order of events and generations. According to them we will never escape the age of the calendar; at most, it will simply start all over again. And in some ways it may even be worse, for how many times will we be doomed to celebrate the centenary of Angioino Tetrastilo?

2. The Tyranny of Time

Calendar-generated culture

Let us now return with renewed confidence to our consideration of the era of the anniversary. If that era is somehow part
of the very order of the cosmos, if indeed it is fated to
continue even after the universal holocaust, then we have no
good reason to abandon the topic.

As I have said, the calendar generates culture by producing
information. It is like a spotlight, picking out people and
events through its mechanism of chronological conjunctions
on a base-ten system. (How different our discussions of
culture would be if our system of numbering were not
decimal! If we counted on a base of three or seven, all our
current anniversaries would go up in smoke and be replaced
by others. Who knows how many new events and celebrities
we would then discover.)

But leaving that question aside, the substance of the
phenomenon I have been describing is as follows: nowadays,
the interest we devote to any person or event that has played
a part in our culture or history is rather like a birthday
present: the French Revolution is 200 years old – Oh my God,
I had better remember to buy it a present! Why does this
happen? The reasons are structural, tied to the way in which
Western civilisation has progressively organised itself for
some two thousand five hundred years. That may seem odd,
at least at first glance, but the modern culture of the anniversary, or rather the supremacy of the calendar, depends
exclusively upon the fact that in Phoenicia at the beginning
of the first millennium BC, someone introduced the alphabet.

Oral culture and the goddess Memory

Before the alphabet the human voice produced culture. By
this I mean that culture was the product of spoken words,

25

exchanged between people once and then lost without a trace, except for the small amount that the memory could retain. The goddess of culture at the time was Mnemosyne, or Memory. It is no coincidence that Hesiod makes Mnemosyne the mother of all the Muses.[6] Hesiod's myth makes sense if you remember that it refers to a world in which poetry was *not written down*; a world in which artistic and philosophical reflection and, above all, its *preservation*, was confined entirely to the small section of the human brain that we call the memory. In a sense, people had their own personal libraries, which they carried around with them. There were advantages to this, but the great disadvantage was that anything that was not remembered was irrevocably lost. Pointless conversations, serious conversations, essential reflections, trivial gossip – all these manifestations of speech shared the common characteristic of vanishing into thin air immediately they had been uttered. When Homer says that someone 'spoke winged words', I think it likely that he did not intend it as a metaphor. In Homer's time, words really did 'fly away' in the sense that it had not yet become general practice to fix them, like butterflies, to a wax tablet – in other words, to write them down.

Our Western culture functioned for centuries within a system of spoken communication. Greece slowly elaborated what we now know as the Homeric poems, the *Iliad* and the *Odyssey*, in predominantly oral form. The Celts, as late as the time of Julius Caesar, handed down their archaic wisdom orally as part of druidic training. It took young apprentices twenty years to learn that wisdom.[7] Caesar does not seem terribly surprised by the fact that the Celts did not write down the most important texts of their civilisation. Perhaps he realised that the Romans had operated in the same way for a long time. When Caesar crossed the Alps and started to write about the unfortunate Celts (as well as conquering them), Rome had had its own written literature for no more than two hundred years. That means, for instance, that the *mos maiorum*, the fundamental code compiled from the precepts of preceding generations and used by every Roman to determine proper behaviour, took shape in the absence of writing. The legends of Romulus and Remus, of Horatius holding the bridge against the Etruscans, of Scaevola who tried to kill Porsenna and then held his right hand in the fire to show his indifference to physical pain, and of Lucretia struggling with the wicked Sextus Tarquinius – these too were all formed in the absence of writing. Even the law, the creative achievement of the Romans that we perhaps admire more than any other, had its roots in a culture in which precedents were handed down from memory and sentences could not be recorded.

The absence of writing clearly does not inhibit the birth or development of civilisation; it simply slows it down. Written texts possess by their very nature an almost blinding speed: once composed, they can immediately be used by other people, who then can write further texts on the basis of their reading, and so on. We even know of texts that have acted like a fuse, triggering by their composition the explosion of an infinite number of further written texts – you have only to think of the Bible or Vergil's *Aeneid*. Nothing comparable could have taken place within a system of purely oral communication where you only have recourse to your own memory or, at most, to the memories of a few trustworthy friends. You cannot go and study in a library. Strictly speaking, in an oral culture you cannot 'study' at all, at least not in the sense in which we use that term today.

If the *Odyssey* had remained sealed within a system of oral communication, no one could have written articles such as 'The Use of the Perfect Tense in the Fourth Book of the Odyssey'. And that is not just because articles are not written in the absence of writing. To start with, we would be unable to identify the 'fourth book' of the *Odyssey* since there would be no single *Odyssey* to refer to but many variant forms of the same epic: the one the epic singer Phemios knew (which is different from the one the epic singer Demodocus knew); the one I heard being recited in the public square the other day; the one my father narrated to me as a child, and so on. And what about the 'perfect tense'? The absence of writing makes it difficult for linguistics to develop, by which I mean the study of language, including grammar. In order to study grammar – dividing and analysing words, comparing them with one another, deducing shared or distinctive traits – you must work from written texts, from objects that you can break up and manipulate; you cannot work from 'winged' words. Linguists have to go back over any text they are studying – but how can you successfully go back over something that has flown away? In an oral culture you cannot even be sure that people are really aware that what they are using are 'words'. Restricting your search to Homer, look for the term he uses for 'word'. You will find that his word, *epos*, does indicate something similar to our 'word', but you will realise that it also means 'speech', 'narration', 'song', and so forth. In an oral context, the word exists as the generic flow of speech; it is not perceived as an isolated element or even one that can be broken down into smaller units. The spoken word, when that is all it is, tends to be somewhat ignorant about itself. Perhaps this is why it seems so delightful and attractive. On the other hand, when the Latin grammarians devoted themselves to phonetics and studied what we today call 'sounds' or, better yet, 'phonemes', they invariably used the word *littera* ('letter') to describe them. Linguistics in the traditional sense is so closely identified with the written word that a linguist wanting to describe 'sounds' is incapable of speaking of anything other than 'letters'.

2. *The Tyranny of Time*

Writing and the archive

The use of writing fixed the word to a tablet once and for all, like a butterfly captured by an entomologist. And we have captured more than just words. The principal virtue of the letters of the alphabet is that they enable us to store any kind of information in the form of tablets, codices, scrolls, books, note cards, electronic files, etc. This fact – the existence of a very powerful memory and one that is, significantly, *outside* us – has changed our way of looking at culture and even our way of looking at memory. If Hesiod were writing his *Theogony* now, he would make the Muses the daughters not of Mnemosyne (Memory) but of Graphe (Writing). No one today could compose any kind of text without a piece of paper and a pen, or a wordprocessor. No one today would ever presume to declare, 'My culture is within me; it is my personal Mnemosyne who preserves and manages it.' Inside us there are fragments, ideas, recollections. Inside us there is the capacity to process what we know or learn. But the place where our culture is preserved and managed is outside us: it is in a library. 'Wait a minute,' you say: 'Hang on while I go and get the *Penal Code*, the computer manual, the *Divine Comedy*, the instructions for the washing machine – *wait until I get a book*.' The library has become our memory – a modest or enormous memory of our personal or collective culture. The library is the modern incarnation of Mnemosyne. From the moment that writing was introduced in Western civilisation, a process of progressive delegation began. We have reduced everything to 'text', transformed everything into letters. Now that memory has moved outside the confines of an individual mind, it has become a truly immense machine.

It is not only recently that this radical process of substitution – reducing our knowledge to text – has taken place. The best description of the process is to be found in a work written fifteen centuries ago, the *Confessions* of St Augustine. I refer to Augustine's splendid description of memory:[8]

> I come to the fields and vast palaces of memory (*et venio in campos et lata praetoria memoriae*), where are the treasuries of innumerable images which have been brought here by sense-perception. Hidden there too is whatever we think about, perhaps increasing or diminishing or in some way altering whatever the senses bring us and whatever else has been deposited or placed in reserve and has not been swallowed up and buried in oblivion. When I come to this place, I ask that it produce what I want, and some things arrive at once; others require a longer search, and it is as if they have to be drawn out from more obscure corners. Others still pour out to crowd the mind and, when one is searching and asking for something quite different, leap forward into the centre as if to say 'Surely we are what you want?' But I chase them away with the hand of my heart from the face of my memory until what I do want is freed of mist and emerges from its hiding place. Other memories come before me on demand with ease and in the order in which they were requested. Memories of earlier events give way to those which followed, and as they pass are stored away, available for retrieval when I want them.

Augustine is speaking of memory, yet he places before us an *archive* – something that very closely resembles a library or even a computer. This is a memory where certain things are 'requested' and this sets off a search procedure. The person performing these mental operations closely resembles a researcher standing at a circulation desk or seated before a flickering screen: 'When I come to this place, I ask that it produce what I want ...' There is even the variation in the length of time you have to wait ('... some things arrive at once; others require a longer search ...'); the accumulation of things brought out by mistake; the presence of those 'more obscure corners' with which older libraries are studded in much the same way as modern hard disks. Augustine speaks of the memory and thinks of an archive; he speaks of images and sees written letters. He is already so completely at home in our modern culture – composed of *litterae*, of symbols that consign knowledge to a place outside ourselves – that, guided by him, we have already entered the place we were bound to enter sooner or later. Without even realising it, we are now inside the vast archive.

Inside the vast archive

So memory has become a library and our culture an archive – a vast archive, to be sure: an enormous collection of files and drawers. We all know that memory operates according to its own particularly arcane laws: these have been investigated by poets, writers and philosophers, and more recently by scientists too. The ancient and medieval art of memory, mnemotechnics, had already transformed the study of memory into a sophisticated discipline.

To find your bearings within your own memory, you turn to the techniques most suited to your needs – or you accept those that nature has bestowed upon you. In any case, everyone knows, or does not know, how to manage the resources of his or her own memory. However, inside archives, especially huge ones, it is a different story.

In order to use any archive, first choose a 'research criterion'; otherwise you are bound to get lost in the stacks. Clearly there is an infinite number of possible research criteria; each scholar must specify his or her own. Let me give a few examples. If your goal is to write an article on the myth of Amphitryon and its variations, your activity inside the archive will be directed towards finding tales of divinities who seduced a woman by assuming the physical appearance of her husband, as Zeus did with Amphitryon's wife, Alcmene; from there you will move on to stories of heroes born from unusual unions, and so on. On the other hand, if you plan to investigate the ways in which an infant learns about colour, you will be guided by a series of completely different criteria marked by stages such as 'infant thought', 'colours', 'names of colours', 'learning', 'psycholinguistics', and so on.

The chronological criterion – that by which we pinpoint an anniversary – is surely the simplest and most immediate of all the criteria for research inside the vast archive. In this case the goal of our research is to establish which great deeds or persons are separated from us by a round number of years. At first glance this might appear a peculiarly mechanical goal, but it does correspond to a serious and deeply felt human need. Here we are, at the centre of this enormous memory/library which we have successfully compiled – what are we to do with all this stuff? How can we determine what is important and what isn't. Above all, how are we to establish what is *real* and what isn't? We surely need a criterion to judge whether Mozart has a right to be performed more often than Boccherini, or *vice versa*; whether it is the Russian Revolution or the Battle of the Piave River that should be the subject of a conference. We have collected all the information, we are ready to discuss it and follow it up, but someone has to tell us what to discuss, what to follow up, and give us a valid reason for doing so.

Given this state of affairs, we have decided to entrust to numbers the task of making choices within the vast archive – always round numbers and especially large numbers. Counting is pretty easy; acquiring the skills of comparative mythology or infant psychology is much more difficult. Look at it this way: in the case of an anniversary one moves in a straightforward linear progression (as exemplified above in the *Conspectus festorum anniversariorum per sigla quadrata*); in the case of comparative mythology or infant learning one orientates oneself a much more complex way.

The anniversary, then, seems an extremely handy criterion of choice. If you find yourself having to determine which composer to retrieve from the vast archive, Mozart or Boccherini, it is much easier to say 'Boccherini' based on the musician's date of birth than to undertake a careful assessment of his musical merits. But this is not enough to explain the success of the anniversary in modern consumer culture. As a criterion of choice it does not recommend itself merely because it is easy; it is attractive primarily because it seems so *objective*. Since the anniversary is based on numbers and calculations it appears to lack controversial or idiosyncratic elements; it derives from *facts*, not opinions. That Boccherini was born in 1743 is an objective incontrovertible fact, just as it is a fact that in 1993 two hundred and fifty years had passed since his birth. In that year it seemed thoroughly appropriate and justifiable to talk about him, to listen to his music, and above all to launch an advertising campaign promoting compact disks and never-previously-released recordings of his quartets for guitar. At least for the duration of this anniversary year, Boccherini's importance to music was so demonstrable that it proved acceptable to the entire community. Professors, lawyers, housewives, taxidrivers – all felt a common bond in acknowledging the need to rank Boccherini ahead of Mozart. Is it his anniversary? – Yes it is, at least until next year which will be characterised by a similar recourse to musical births or deaths, equally factual and equally acceptable to all.

The personification of anniversaries

Cultural activity regulated by anniversary – handy, objective, acceptable to all – is thus very useful from the point of view of its relationship to *consumerism*. Most people find it perfectly natural to take an interest in something because it is separated from us by a round number of years. We are accustomed to the need to remember, without fail, the birthday of a spouse, St Valentine's Day, or Mother's Day. Our lives exhibit a striking penchant for anniversaries. As we all know, we can expect moral and familial sanctions if we miss them.

Both St Valentine's Day and Mother's Day necessitate the existence of a person. Mother's Day is concerned with a person: your mother. St Valentine's Day presupposes the existence of a saint, but also that of a girlfriend or boyfriend whose tastes and desires you have to take into account. During such a celebration, for example a birthday, it is the biographical reality of someone else that becomes your focus of attention: you are saying: 'Look, I remembered you' and the person whose birthday it is responds: 'It's my birthday, let's talk about me.'

On a Roman's *dies natalis* (birthday) the celebrations consisted of making gifts and sacrifices to the *genius* or *iuno*[9] (the divine manifestation) of the person being honoured. The Romans had a more religious view of their place in the world than we do: they did not use concepts such as 'personality', 'self' and 'ego' to give form to their personal identity. The *genius* or *iuno* was a god, though admittedly a minor one, and on one's birthday that god was to be celebrated. There is no better way to emphasise that the *person* is necessarily the centre of attention each time the day of celebration comes round.

Let us return to the anniversary. The analogy with birthdays, Mother's Day and St Valentine's Day leads us at last to the following significant conclusion: any historical event or product of human ingenuity, once it has been subjected to the regime of the anniversary, tends to become 'personified'.

2. The Tyranny of Time

It is no longer a question of something but of someone. When the French Revolution 'is two hundred years old', as we heard over and over again on the anniversary, or when the so-called discovery of America 'is five hundred years old', these historical events seem to become personified. It is as if we recognise them, without saying so explicitly, as living, animate beings.

In ancient rhetoric there was a specific technical term to describe this process: *prosopopoeia* (in Latin, *conformatio*), a rhetorical device by which inanimate objects or abstract ideas are made to speak and act.[10] A striking example is found in Cicero's first speech against Catiline, where the mighty Roman Republic (*res publica*) herself turns to address Cicero:

> Marcus Tullius, what are you doing? This man is a public enemy, as you have discovered; he will be the leader of the war, as you see; men are waiting for him to take command in the enemies' camp, as you know; author of a crime, head of a conspiracy, recruiter of slaves and criminals – and you will let him go, in such a way that he will seem to be not cast out of the city by you but let loose against the city![11]

She goes on in similar vein, uttering her 'most solemn ... words' (*sanctissimae voces*) for at least three more paragraphs. And the privilege of personification was not the sole preserve of majestic or venerable entities such as the Republic. At times it happened to less solemn subjects such as 'mountains, rivers, trees'.[12] So one should be not be surprised by the fact that America, in 1992, raised itself up from beyond the ocean and shouted at Genoa: 'What are you doing, birthplace of Christopher Columbus? Are you going to let this year slip by without budget appropriations ...?'

This continual *prosopopoeia* or personification of our cultural past is not an isolated or accidental phenomenon. On the contrary, it is very much in keeping with the direction our culture has taken in recent times. We have all become much more accustomed to dealing with 'people' than with abstract ideas or the historical interpretation of events. At the very least, when discussing ideas or events we much prefer to have a tangible point of reference. We live in the age of television, a means of communication which inevitably brings the person into the foreground. Television functions as a unique, inexhaustible personifier. In a culture dominated by television, there is no doubt that events and ideas are important, but their protagonists are even more important. The talk-show feeds insatiably off people who are considered (very often erroneously) to be protagonists of some sort, but even news programmes and special reports usually operate in the same way. Moreover the conventions of film, and especially soap opera, have greatly accelerated a process already present in traditional fiction: the process by which debates about important cultural issues – love, professional ethics, family relationships – seem ever more closely tied to specific individuals. Will the rekindled romance between ER's Doctor Ross and Nurse Hathaway lead to a permanent relationship? Serious examination of our culture increasingly takes the form of a narrative, and the 'theme' of the discussion is invariably a person.

That is why a culture like ours, when it comes face to face with the so-called discovery of America, immediately produces a vast number of narratives (films, biographies, radio dramas) which bring the 'protagonists' of that series of events into the foreground, so that we can personify our history. The event itself was chosen for notice in exactly the same way, using a criterion that is just as 'personal' – the anniversary. The discovery of America is five hundred years old, so let's celebrate its *person*, let's transform the event into a series of personal histories. If we continue in this way, there is a risk that the vast archive will end up looking less like a

2. The Tyranny of Time

library and more like a retirement home for personages of the past. We thought they were dead, but it turns out that they are still very much alive and willing to be interviewed.

3

The Urge for Instant Gratification

The essential buzz

It is always good to begin with words. That is the golden rule
of philology, which comes from the ancient Greek for 'a love
of words'. Beautiful or ugly, modern or old-fashioned – all
words bear witness to the culture that produced them, and
can often reveal its deepest inclinations.

In our culture the words of the moment are all to do with
'fun', 'entertainment', 'pleasure' and 'excitement'. Thrill-
seeking is the ultimate goal of our society, pleasure is the
highest good. Even a recent article I wrote on Latin metre
– not the most stimulating of topics, you might think –
came back from friends to whom I had sent it with
comments such as 'I very much enjoyed this', 'Very enter-
taining' or even 'I loved the way you dealt with Plautus'
metre'. And in our culture these are the highest forms of
praise. We have made enjoyment our dominant criterion of
evaluation, and as a result we subordinate many other
criteria to it.

Pleasure, in all its linguistic guises, should always be
present in our cultural activity. If you are going on a trip,
even a trip to learn a foreign language, it must be motivated
by 'enjoyment'. I will only go to Turkey if I am guaranteed to
have fun in Istanbul, if it is an 'exciting' or 'beautiful' city;
similarly, I will only dedicate myself to the study of German
as long as I 'enjoy' my relationship with separable verbs. In
order to move around inside the vast archive of culture, the

impulse must come to me from that specific area of the brain that controls sensations of pleasure.

In Italian the word for this 'pleasure-impulse' is *sfizio*, and this will be a key word in my analysis of contemporary culture. The Italian adjective derived from it, *sfizioso*, is very much in vogue at the moment (indicative, I believe, of our culture's inclinations). It can be translated into English as 'exciting', 'arousing', 'enticing', 'giving a buzz'; but there is far more to it than that, as will become clear below. The *sfizio* is a craving or impulse that must be satisfied immediately, and ours is the era of instant gratification, the age of the *sfizio*, the 'buzz'.

Getting a buzz from etymologies

In the city where I live there is a large bar called 'Lo Sfizio'. It is an attractive place, brightly lit, providing all sorts of enticing snacks to go with your drink – crisps, peanuts, olives, thin slices of prosciutto, paprika-flavoured popcorn .... Clearly, if you pop into Bar Sfizio you are satisfying the urge of the moment. In Italian the phrase used to describe this activity is 'cavarsi uno sfizio', where *cavarsi* means 'to remove' – the same word is used for extracting a tooth. It seems to me no coincidence that *cavarsi* is used in both cases – in fact, it deserves closer analysis. As I have said before, it is always a good idea to begin with words and their meanings.

So let us take a closer look. The *sfizio* – the impulse or craving – cannot in itself be a pleasurable sensation. It has to be removed, implying that it causes discomfort while you have it and that the pleasure is a consequence of its removal. It confirms the ancient theory that pleasure is nothing more than the absence of pain. As Epicurus said, 'When we say that our goal is pleasure ... we mean ... freedom from physical pain

39

and from disturbance of the soul.'[1] But this is philosophy. Philology, on the other hand, requires more detailed research and further clarification.

Strangely, Italian dictionaries do not supply a standard etymology for the word *sfizio*. They note that the expression originated in southern Italy and then spread throughout the country.[2] But we might have guessed that anyway: a word like *sfizio* immediately evokes the south – sunshine and coffee. We feel instinctively that 'impulses' are experienced more frequently in southern Italy. At this point readers from southern climes are probably saying to themselves 'Of course! What sort of impulses could be satisfied in the north anyway, where it's so gloomy and cold.' Yet nowadays even northerners act on impulse, even if they haven't quite got the hang of it yet. And perhaps even southerners do not fully appreciate quite what it means to remove a *sfizio*. Under the entry *sfizziu*, Giuseppe L. Messina writes as follows:

> Here is a word that is not included in most dictionaries, but the Sicilians use it frequently and have it in common with the Neapolitans (*sfizio*), the Abruzzesi (*sfizie*) and the Calabrians (*sfizziu*). Depending on context, it can mean 'desire, wish, whim, pleasure, satisfaction', with the implication of a deep pleasure in having done or said – or in the anticipation of doing or saying – something that may be frivolous or even objectively distasteful. The verb *sfizziàrsi* (meaning to have fun, to satisfy a craving) derives from *sfizziu*. Its etymology is obscure.[3]

This obscurity does not bode well. We live in the age of the *sfizio*, yet we do not even know what we are removing when we carry out one of the principal rituals that govern our culture.

Let us continue with our analysis of the word, which, incidentally, is not a particularly attractive one – in fact it is quite ugly. However, a good philologist must disregard matters of taste: all words are equal. Even Professor Messina attests that a *sfizio* can at times be associated with something that is 'objectively distasteful'. We had already arrived at this conclusion independently by analysing the verb that normally accompanies *sfizio* in Italian, i.e. *cavarsi*, 'to remove'. In Italian, another word that goes with *cavarsi* – another thing that we remove, apart from *sfizii* and teeth, is *voglia* ('craving' or 'desire'). Thus one might drop into the Bar Sfizio to *cavarsi la voglia* ('indulge one's craving') for a glass of wine or a chocolate eclair. We have taken another important step forward. *Sfizio* is synonymous with craving (*voglia*). It is just that we are more used to the anthropological discussion of 'cravings' and 'desires' than of *sfizii*. We know about cravings, when they occur and to whom. We know that they are traditionally attributed to pregnant women, who at dead of night may be seized by a craving for strawberries or fried potatoes. According to traditional folklore these cravings must be satisfied or the unborn child may be disfigured by a birthmark on the cheek or a crooked yellow nose. Naturally, such cravings are usually for foods that are particularly rare and expensive: exotic fruit, caviar and smoked salmon (before we started farming salmon). Cravings are historically located, and follow fads and changes in the market. For example, in the eighteenth century there was a great (and often unsatisfied) craving for coffee and chocolate. What else can explain the abundance of facial moles that characterised that era?[4]

Anyway, we have taken another important step forward. If an unsatisfied craving can be manifested as a birthmark or physical defect in an unborn child, we can see why cravings *must* be removed, just like a tooth or a gangrenous limb. Cravings are part of the body; they must be got rid of by consuming the appropriate food.

41

No one should underestimate the importance of cravings in the evolution of civilisation. The great James Frazer identified them as the origin of the elusive phenomenon that anthropologists call 'totemism'.[5] His sources informed him that in Melanesia it was believed that the life of an individual was linked to that of a particular animal or plant. The choice of these external spirits was made solely on the basis of the fancies of the mother when she was pregnant. Frazer had no doubts: totemism as a phenomenon derives from the cravings of pregnant women. Frazer probably exaggerated and placed too much importance on the alimentary whims that he observed in Victorian women, for once in their lives authorised by pregnancy to express their repressed longings. One thing is certain, though. The ancients were well aware of the existence of cravings, a phenomenon discussed at length in the classics.

The Latin word for craving is *incies*, which probably alludes to the stirring (*cieo*, *ciere*) which moves a pregnant women when her cravings make themselves felt. In other words, the craving is an impulse, an irrepressible urge that comes from within: clearly it must be placated and calmed or the woman suffers and the unborn child runs the risk of being indelibly marked by all this anxiety. The Greeks, on the other hand, used an unexpected word, *kissa*. This is the name of a bird, the magpie. But what does the magpie have to do with cravings? The explanation lies in its habits and popular beliefs surrounding them. The magpie has a reputation for being a thief and a glutton, and in particular for stealing shiny objects. As an ancient commentator on Aristophanes explained, the craving of a pregnant woman is called *kissa* because 'the magpie is a gluttonous bird that eats a lot, and it is just as voracious in its desires'.[6] To cut a long story short, a craving is a magpie because it is like a bird with its beak wide open, a truly gluttonous creature. The pattern is the same: the 'agitation' of the craving-*incies* must be placated immediately; the craving-magpie needs to be satisfied, driven off. It is not much fun having cravings; it is best to remove them as quickly as possible.

What about the *sfizio*? In ancient Greek there is a verb, *sphyzo*, which means 'to beat' in the sense of 'to pulsate' (like a heart).[7] It is found in the technical terms sphygmo-manometer, sphygmograph, and so on, which describe the instruments used by doctors to measure pulse and record the pulse. *Sphyzo* may well be the origin of our *sfizio*, for it also means 'to be agitated', 'to be upset', and, more relevantly, 'to desire something strongly'. We're there: a *sfizio* is closely associated with strong desire and craving. There is also another word with the same root, *sphygmos*, which can describe a state of strong psychological agitation. By now the metaphorical process by which 'throbbing' becomes 'desire' should be familiar. A strong desire is perceived as an 'impulse', a 'throbbing pulse', which we have also met when speaking of the *incies*, or the 'stirring' which affected preg-nant Roman women. A *sfizio* is an agitation, an uncomfortable sensation of 'throbbing' inside, from which you must free yourself as quickly as possible. That explains why a *sfizio* must be removed like an aching tooth.

Getting our kicks

Etymologies can be great fun. As Leo Spitzer said, 'Studying words is a pleasure' ('Es ist eine Lust, Wortforscher zu sein'). The German word *Lust* ('pleasure') also means 'craving', as in English. To investigate a word *is* to gratify an impulse, especially when that word is *sfizio*. Satisfying as etymologies are, however, we must now return to our own culture. It is the culture of the *sfizio*; a culture that pursues the kicks which come from gratifying cravings; a culture of continual throbbing pulses and itches. It is the culture of the agitated pregnancy and of the voracious magpie, created by people whose greatest concern is with soothing, or more precisely with 'removing', every slightest urge or itch. I am well aware that I have reached this conclusion in a rather metaphorical way by analysing words that seem to have almost nothing to do with the sociology of contemporary communication. And yet it all seems to work: philology teaches us to rely on words.

If you go into a bookshop and buy a copy of *William Tell* by Schiller for a few pounds, what are you doing but indulging a sudden impulse, soothing the *incies*, driving off the magpie which has unexpectedly stirred inside you. The same goes for a manual such as *Have Fun and Learn to Play the Guitar in Only Ten Lessons*. And it is also the impulse behind an expression one often hears on television: the interviewer turns to the expert and says, 'Can you explain continental drift in just a few words?' If the expert attempts to expand on the subject with an explanation that is not sufficiently simplistic, he or she will be immediately interrupted (that's enough – we've chased away the magpie of continental drift – your few words were quite sufficient). For a brief moment the interviewer felt that the viewers must be in the grip of an irresistible impulse to know more about continental drift; a few words from an expert were imperative. But now the moment is past; other more urgent desires need to be satisfied with 'just a few words'.

We are about to learn philology's final and by no means insignificant lesson: in the lexicon of television, the *sfizio* is the 'few words', the 'soundbite'. The phrase 'tell us in just a few words' is capable of transforming the most complicated of subjects into a *sfizio*, an itch that needs to be scratched. The interviewer probably doesn't realise it, but when she says, for example, 'Professor, in a few words, prove to us that God exists', she is acting like a pregnant woman with a craving for *foie gras* in a railway buffet. But it is not her fault; the problem lies elsewhere. It is the audience that suffers from *sphyzein*: they are the ones aroused by every form of *incies*. The audience is an insatiable magpie.

Symbolising the buzz

Ancient civilisations made an art of linking specific cultural or religious attributes with particular plants. For instance, laurel was generally associated with victory, while an oak leaf evoked courage in battle. The olive tree symbolised peace and myrtle, a plant sacred to Venus, evoked love. Fig leaves were usually associated with fertility, wild lavender with chastity. Even the most humble plant could secure its place in the symbolic universe of ancient civilisations. Celery, for instance, was associated with victory in athletic competitions and sometimes with banqueting, while basil was linked to profanity, which may seem a little odd to us today. Pliny suggested that the planting of basil should be accompanied by 'curses and imprecations' to ensure abundant growth.[8] Even the squill (*scilla*) – a bitter bulb which produces a small hyacinth-like flower, known as *lampascione* in southern Italy where it is considered a delicacy – had its own meaning: it symbolised periods of famine, scarcity and foraging, and the ancients accorded it healing powers when used in certain rituals.[9]

Traces of such ancient symbolic plant classifications survive in our own culture. They are preserved in the works of art that still adorn our historic buildings or stand in our museums ('Why has that statue got laurel on his head?') so that we are still aware to some extent that laurel stands for victory or that the olive branch evokes peace. It is not just a question of ruins and remains, however. Many people are aware that red roses symbolise love, while yellow roses mean jealousy. People are still unlikely to plant cypress trees in their gardens, for the cypress symbolises death and burial, just as it did in Roman times. So we clearly still attribute certain meanings to plants or link them into certain cultural rituals. We may well ask, then, whether one of the main ritual practices of our age, the satisfaction of the *sfizio*, has a symbolic equivalent in the plant world. If the laurel recalls victory and the cypress death, what evokes the sudden impulse?

I have no hesitation in answering 'Rocket!' There is no better plant to associate with the *sfizio*. Its peppery leaf is becoming more and more popular as a way of livening up all sorts of bland dishes, not just salads but cold meats, bresaola, carpaccio, steak, pasta sauces. Nowadays rocket has even begun to make its appearance on that staple of Italian food, the pizza. Given the important role of the pizza in Italian society, it needs a bit of a 'kick'. These days all sorts of unexpected things turn up on pizzas, from artichoke hearts to herring, from mussels to smoked ham. In Italian pizzerias the menu has become an interminable sacred litany with a refrain that sends you into ecstasies: pizza with ... pizza with ... pizza with .... The pizza is the perfect symbol of the magpie 'pick and mix' society, and it is no surprise that we have begun to scatter rocket on our pizzas.

Rocket has all the characteristics of the *sfizio*: it stimulates, it arouses desire. Its strong peppery flavour generates that throbbing, or *sphygmos*, which we know is at the heart of this experience. Rocket is used sparingly – you would never eat an entire bowlful – to kick-start the tastebuds. It not only delivers a kick itself, it livens up any dish to which it is added. That is its principal virtue, explaining its success in contemporary cuisine. Rocket brightens up the boring ritual of family meals or fast food, adding an essential spark of excitement which none of us today seems willing to forego. It has become obligatory to indulge impulses, whether interviewing someone on television, studying German, or even writing an article on classical metre. How can we do without excitement at mealtimes too?

Deifying the buzz

The ancient classification of plants is fascinating, each plant being part of an endlessly complex network of associations and connotations. Let us take as an example the ritual of the Bona Dea (Good Goddess), an ancient Roman cult celebrated by women which exalted the virtues of chastity and sobriety – the qualities that the Romans associated with the ideal *matrona* (married woman). Men were strictly excluded from this cult – not only flesh and blood men but even depictions of men. If there were any male statues or figurines in the home, they were covered up. Even male animals were not supposed to be present during the ritual. Since women were not allowed to drink wine in ancient Rome, it was banned from the cult; instead there were foods considered more in keeping with the feminine, such as milk and honey. All sorts of plants were involved in the ritual, but strictly *not* the myrtle plant. The explanation is simple: myrtle was sacred to the goddess of love, Venus, and for that reason was not suitable for a celebration of chastity. In addition, its small bunches of berries were similar to those of the grape vine, so it would have suggested the unlawful presence of grapes and wine at the ritual. In the language of plants, the presence of myrtle at the Bona Dea would have been the equivalent of a swear word or an obscene gesture.

At the centre of such symbolic networks there is always a divinity who embodies the religious essence that a culture expresses through plants, foodstuffs, ritual activities, and so on. In the case of myrtle, as we have seen, the divinity was

Venus, while Apollo was the god of laurel, Jupiter the god of oak, and so on. Even seeds had their own divinities. St Augustine explains that, in ancient Roman religion, seeds were divided into two groups: 'liquid' and 'solid'.[10] The god Liber ruled over 'liquid' or 'moist' seeds, while Ceres ruled over 'solid' or 'dry' seeds.[11] But at this point the classification of plants intersected dangerously with animals and sex – one of Augustine's pet hates. The liquid seeds were divided in turn into two sub-groups: those that come from animals (seminal liquids) and those that come from plants. Strangely, we find that wine is a member of the former group. All the liquid seeds of which the god Liber was master shared one trait: they were strictly masculine. So for the ancient Romans wine was a liquid seed that was *masculine*; it belonged to the same group as the semen produced by men. And this may explain why Roman women could not drink wine: it would have been like drinking semen. Liber, god of liquid seeds, controlled a remarkable symbolic network.

Unravelling all the different associations of rocket in our own system of classification would be very difficult. Our culture seems to have greatly reduced – at least on a conscious level – the length of the symbolic chains connected to our social rituals. Besides, we have no divinities with whom to associate our favourite plants. We know that rocket is a plant linked to excitement and impulse – the *sfizio*. But who can say whether it is a masculine plant rather than a feminine one? Or that it goes with wine rather than milk? We are unlikely to be found explaining to our waiter that we do not want a pizza with rocket not because we don't like it but because we are not worshippers of the god Rocket. Fortunately the classification of plants in antiquity can partly compensate for our deficiencies and help us rediscover a number of associations and meanings that have not been entirely lost.

3. The Urge for Instant Gratification

The Romans described at some length the power and significance of rocket, which they called *eruca*. The evidence is very clear on one aspect: *eruca* was closely associated with male sexuality and was considered a powerful aphrodisiac for men.[12] So firmly rooted was this conviction that Ovid, who in his *Remedies for Love* tended to be very practical, advised men who wished to free themselves of the tyranny of lust never to eat rocket.[13] So the excitement that rocket on a pizza or in a salad arouses in men is a sexual one. Are the customers of pizzerias aware of this? Let us move on. Pliny the Elder, arguing that 'the reproductive urge may also be stimulated by foodstuffs', offers the examples of rocket for a man and onion for a goat.[14] In other words, what rocket is for men, onion is for goats (without wishing to offend those who like onion on their pizza, of whom there are plenty). Pliny continues: 'rocket, since it is unaffected by cold, is the complete opposite of lettuce (*lactuca*), and it is capable of exciting sexual desire; thus it is usually added to a salad of lettuce so that the excessive coldness of the lettuce may be tempered and counterbalanced by the heat of rocket.'[15]

So the polar opposite of rocket is lettuce. Rocket, because of its peppery flavour and aphrodisiacal effect on men, belongs at the 'hot' end of the spectrum, while lettuce is 'cold'. Pliny's words also imply that lettuce, as the inverse of rocket, does the opposite of arousing erotic passion. Other sources are more explicit on this point. Lettuce was indeed considered an anti-aphrodisiac for men,[16] food for the impotent and for corpses.[17] Frigid anti-erotic lettuce is exactly the opposite of a stimulating and exciting (*sfiziosa*) plant. The Romans attributed digestive and laxative properties to lettuce,[18] and it was said that the emperor Augustus was saved because his doctor, Musa, wisely administered lettuce to cure his liver disease.[19] Lettuce is a medicine, not a delicacy. Furthermore the Latin word for lettuce, *lactuca*,

49

contains the word 'milk' (*lact-*), as the ancients liked to point out. Its veins are milky, as you will find if you tear off a leaf. Milk is not an arousing substance, conjuring up as it does images of infancy and the mother's breast. Milk is bland; it has no 'kick'. So milk too, along with lettuce, cold and sexual abstinence, is part of the symbolic army marshalled against rocket.

To complete the picture, we still have to identify the god of rocket. I suspect some of you already have your suspicions! Columella explicitly tells us in his treatise on farming that in a garden rocket is sown 'beside fertile Priapus'.[20] For a herb that stimulates sexual arousal in men, the associated divinity could hardly be other than Priapus himself – the god with a large erect phallus who in Roman gardens performed a function not unlike that of the scarecrow in our fields today, warding off evil from a cultivated area. He had a number of characteristics, in particular a tendency to blatant exhibitionism with which our culture would certainly not be comfortable. Priapus is the god Rocket, and the devout consumers of *eruca* address him silently in prayer.[21]

There you have it – a brief description of the plant we have become accustomed to add to a variety of dishes for a bit of excitement. Rocket is still a 'hot', 'masculine' plant linked with male sexuality and ruled by the phallic god Priapus. Might these characteristics in any way have influenced the remarkable success that this little plant is now enjoying? Do these characteristics correspond to any prevailing trends in our era? I believe that the answer is Yes. Our culture is driven by impulses that are to some extent sexual. The revelations and surprises that, as you will see, we spring upon ourselves, are sexual and specifically concerned with male sexuality. In the chapters that follow it will become clear that my examples are frequently concerned with just this theme. Glossy magazines, television, films and novels are most liberal in scattering the 'rocket' of sex on the dishes they serve up to their customers. At least on the cover, a little rocket goes very well, helping to make the financial pages inside a bit more palatable. Perhaps we have lived too long in the anti-aphrodisiacal era of lettuce. Now we are chasing the cold away. This is the age of Viagra!

Getting a buzz out of the classics

In and of themselves, the classics are not at first glance very exciting. At least it would be difficult to argue that Cicero's *Republic* or Vergil's *Aeneid* are 'a lot of fun'. The classics have their appeal, no doubt, but they tend to be serious, sometimes even downright austere. Not all of them, of course: we can still read Petronius' *Satyricon* or the *Priapic Poems*. But there are few such examples, and it would be difficult to build an entire 'Library of Excitement' from the classics. Yet it is true that exciting editions of Petronius and the *Priapic Poems* have multiplied in recent times, perhaps under the influence of the Age of Rocket. Indeed the god Priapus is one of the principal heroes of the *Satyricon*. We might have expected greater success for Lucian's *A True Story* or Apuleius' *Metamorphoses* (also known as *The Golden Ass*),[22] but not for Greek novels in general: once you start reading them you soon realise that there is little arousing in them; they are even more boring than 'Beverly Hills 90210'.

The classical tradition has been less than generous in supplying literature of an exciting nature. For instance, Aristides of Miletus' *Milesian Tales* have not come down to us. If they had, we would certainly be in better shape: there is evidence that the Romans packed this book in their baggage for Crassus' campaign against the Parthians,[23] which might help to explain why they were defeated at the battle of Carrhae. After their victory, the Parthians mocked the

51

Romans, 'since they could not, even when they were going to war, let such subjects and writing alone'. The taunting of the victors confirms that the *Milesian Tales* must have been pretty stimulating stuff. What a shame that we no longer have them! And the gap certainly cannot be filled by Macrobius' *Saturnalia*. It is a nice title: saturnalian, carnivalesque, evoking images of drunken slaves, well-endowed scantily dressed women and the worship of bodily pleasures. But Macrobius' *Saturnalia* is in fact an austere treatise on the interpretation of Vergil with a decided penchant for antiquarian scholarship.

Stimulating extracts

Although the thoroughly 'enjoyable' classics are few, we still have the option of chopping them up to reveal their most arousing parts, in a slick operation of editorial 'cut and paste'. For instance, you could assemble a short volume entitled *The Erotica of Lucretius*, putting together a careful selection of passages from the fourth book of his *De rerum natura* (though Lucretius actually deals with ejaculation in a very serious way); or you could collect a juicy anthology of insults, affronts and invective drawn from the principal authors of Roman literature.[24] But if you decide to cut and paste from the comedies of Plautus, expecting them to be an inexhaustible mine of vulgarities and obscenities, I advise you not to draw your material from the Latin text but from one of the modern translations, in which there are far more insults and obscenities than in the original. The point is that Plautus, that raw poet of the people, considered a forerunner of the Italian poet Belli and admired by Pier Paolo Pasolini,[25] almost never used swear words and rarely allowed himself obscene allusions. You can imagine the disappointment of his recent translators.

3. The Urge for Instant Gratification

Surely a selection of Martial's epigrams would be enough to get us excited? Well, in Italy we have indeed recently seen the publication of a short volume entitled *Martial: The One Hundred Censored Epigrams*, in the 'Millelire' series.[26] Just who these epigrams were censored by is not at all clear, but it is a good publicity ploy by those at the Millelire press: marketed in this way, Martial's poems immediately become as enticing and arousing as those erotic Pompeian frescoes that the guide allows only certain tourists to see (generally those who reward him handsomely). What they see, of course, are images of Priapus, who remained erect right up to the volcanic eruption, or of shapely women, all set against a background of mould and flaking plaster. Millelire books certainly have a flair for publishing titles that sound stimulating. Let me give you another example. Suppose you were translating Cicero's *De senectute* for a popular series of inexpensive paperbacks. How would you render the title? *Old Age* is a title with limited appeal. *Great Age* is even less enticing, suggesting that Cicero had written a book on Methuselah and his older brothers. Millelire books pulled off a brilliant coup: *De senectute* became *L'arte di invecchiare* (*The Art of Growing Old*). There cannot be many who do not want to learn that art.

The power (and perils) of quotation

There is one swift and sure way to make any classic exciting: quotation. Quotation pares the classic down to its bare bones, reducing it to something so slight that it cannot help but be tantalising and intriguing. This explains why so many collections of quotations are published nowadays. There are now so many such anthologies that they have a section to themselves in bookshops. Through quotation a classic becomes so small that it can be encompassed in a soundbite, those 'few words' that, as we have seen, comprise the televisual equivalent of a *sfizio*. Here are a few examples:

Interviewer: Horace, in a few words, your opinion of Danilus Poggiolinus?[27]

Horace: He has set up a monument more lasting than bronze (*Exegit monumentum aere perennius*, *Carmina* 3.30.1).

Interviewer: Augustus (*on his death bed*), in a few words, your opinion of Giulio Andreotti?

Augustus (*close to death*): The farce has played itself out (*Acta est fabula*, cf. Suetonius, *Divus Augustus* 99.1).[28]

Interviewer: Vergil, in a few words, your opinion of artificial insemination and late motherhood?

Vergil: Seek out your ancient mother (*Antiquam exquirite matrem*, *Aeneid* 3.96).

Interviewer: And your views on the national debt?

Vergil: Your children's children shall gather your fruits (*Carpent tua poma nepotes*, *Eclogues* 9.50).

Interviewer: And of public sponsorship of political parties?

Vergil: Shut off the streams now, my boys, the meadows have drunk enough (*Claudite iam rivos, pueri, sat prata biberunt*, *Eclogues* 3.111).

Used in such a way the classics can be fun and contemporary. Presented like this, we may note that the classics become almost proverbial, taking on an autonomous circulation, a collective paternity and an anonymous authorship. *Senectus ipsa est morbus* (Old age is a disease in itself): nice saying, but who wrote it? That doesn't matter; all that is important is that it is in Latin. To be in Latin is to be by someone, or rather, by Someone. Latin is classic in its own right. It is as though it were a de-personalised, collective Super-Author, automatically great simply for being Latin. The words in

3. The Urge for Instant Gratification

Latin quotations assume their form as though they were an entirely self-generating language, which has slipped from the hands of its lawful owners and is liable to the most extraordinary misunderstandings.

The buzz of Latin puzzles

The Latin of quotations, whether accurate or not, has the air of a perfect language. At the very least it seems a logical language, as we were assured at school when we did not want to study it: learn to study Latin, which is a logical language, and you will do well in mathematics too. This was held to be so self-evidently true that if you were doing well in mathematics and badly in Latin, or *vice versa*, the teachers became suspicious and summoned your parents: the disparity made no sense; something else must be up, such as politics or sex. It is true that the Latin we learned at school is (or perhaps was) a perfect language. You could play with it as though it were a puzzle; break it apart and put it back together in an endless game. Take the fact that Latin words often have, in addition to their primary meaning, an infinite number of other meanings that spark off from the first with irresistible, irrefutable logic. This becomes clear in the case of anagrams.[29]

Take, for example, the word *digitus* ('finger' or 'thumb'). Rearrange the letters and you have a child and the behaviour he has now grown out of: *digitus* becomes *id sugit* ('he sucked it'). When the thumbsucker grows up and begins to study philosophy, it is immediately clear why philosophical reasoning proves so difficult and obscure: *logica* ('logic') becomes *caligo* ('fog'). But the great philosophers turn out to be readily comprehensible in Latin: Democritus becomes *mire doctus* ('wonderfully learned'); Epicurus becomes *vir pecus* ('sheep man', with his famous 'flock') and so on, except

55

for some uncertainty about Socrates, who could appear in the solemn guise of *sto sacer* ('I am sacred') or in the somewhat more rhetorical one of *os sacret* ('let the mouth immortalise'). Socrates is as mysterious in anagrams as in life, when he mystified his followers by insisting on taking hemlock to end his life rather than escaping with his friend Crito. In fact, Democritus too can appear both as *mire doctus* and as one who *docet risum* ('teaches laughter'). His name thus indicates not only the quality of his teaching but also the legend that at some point in his life he fell prey to uncontrollable laughter. 'O Hippocrates,' wrote the people of Abdera to the most famous doctor of the day, 'a most grave danger overshadows our city.' Democritus, the pride and joy of Abdera, seemed to have lost his mind. Day and night he stayed awake 'finding everything, great and small, hilariously funny, and maintaining that one's entire life amounted to nothing'.[30] But when Hippocrates went to Abdera he was forced to acknowledge that Democritus' laughing fits in fact comprised the philosopher's noblest teaching. *Democritus – docet risum*.

The fund of wisdom hidden in Latin words is inexhaustible. You only have to scratch the surface and you discover, for example, why language emerges from the mouth: *lingua* ('language') becomes *in gula* ('in the throat'). And when a boy first experiences sexual arousal, Latin warns him off: *femina* ('woman') becomes *infame* ('disreputable'), *copula* ('intercourse') becomes *pocula* ('cups' or 'potions'), *virgo* ('virgin') becomes *vigor* ('strength'), and even *osculum* ('kiss') becomes *musculo* ('for a little mouse'). We have wise anagrams from the Bible: *Pilatus*: *'Quid est veritas?' Christus: 'Vir qui adest.'* (Pilate: 'What is truth?' Christ: 'The man who stands before you.') As for Peter, it is no surprise that he denied his master three times: *O Petrus!* becomes *Proteus* ('fickle'). And since the Jesuits must have their say we must include their founder's anagram: *Ignatius de Loyola* becomes *O ygnis il(l)atus a deo* ('O fire ignited by God!').

Latin has this unique virtue: it offers words which simultaneously present themselves and their explanation. That should come as no surprise given that Latin is such a perfect language that it makes use only of words connected to the thing they describe by a tie of complete and absolute necessity. This is a great advantage because it bypasses the trouble caused by the 'arbitrariness of the sign' (to use an expression of Saussure's[31]) which leads to awkward questions such as 'Why is a wife called a "wife" and not a "wharf" or even a "bottle"?' In Latin that sort of question would never come up, for every word in Latin is justifiable. For instance, a wife is called *uxor* in Latin because *Uae notat U, crucis est X symbolon, O facit ira, Rque canes diro littera dente decet.* That is: 'the U stands for "woe to...", the X is the symbol of the cross, O implies anger, and the letter R ("rrrr...!") comes from growling dogs with vicious fangs.' The explanation itself is in the form of an elegiac couplet, which is the most you possibly could hope for. A shame that Latin was such a misogynistic language!

Even the declension of nouns, through endings that you had to learn in order to determine whether the action involved several *puellae* in the nominative plural, or only one *puella* but in the dative or genitive case – even these cases in the final analysis are thoroughly justifiable. When the devil conducted a lesson in hell for his little demons, he explained to them how the cases in Latin functioned:

Remember the Nominative by the *superbos* ('the proud who lord it over others')

The Genitive by the *libidinosus* ('the libidinous who do their generating by copulation')

The Dative by the *prodigos* ('the spendthrifts who give recklessly to others')

The Accusative by the *calumniatores* ('the calumniators who falsely accuse others')

The Ablative by the *fures et raptores* ('the thieves and robbers who take away from others')

So there is no escaping Latin cases, even after death: they are transformed into the most complicated, bureaucratic bedlam straight out of Dante and used to organise the entire land-scape of hell, where libidinous Genitives and thieving Ablatives are punished. Perfection usually has another side – severity. And Latin is (or was) a language as perfect as it is severe, especially when it comes to learning the irregular nouns of the third declension that have the accusative in *-im* and the ablative in *-i*: *iussis, amussis, vis, burris* etc. Heinrich Heine presents himself as a willing witness: as a child, he never succeeded in memorising them. In fact little Heinrich, spending his entire morning in front of a crucified Christ in grey wood ('a dismal image that even now at times walks through my dreams and sadly looks at me with fixed, bleeding eyes') used to pray: 'O thou, poor God, equally tormented, if it at all possible, see that I keep the irregular nouns in my head!'[32]

Classic abridgements

Let us return to the potential of Latin to excite us. A further technique of arousal, similar to anthology and quotation, is abridgement. Neatly summarised, the classics can be stripped of their most boring and austere parts so that we can enjoy their most exciting and pleasurable elements. For instance, you could take out of the *Iliad* all those battles and councils of the gods which serve no real purpose and summarise them thus: 'There was a war in what is now Anatolia in which several of the leading gods were involved.' You can thus

3. The Urge for Instant Gratification

emphasise the parts where, for example, human brain squirts from a crushed skull, which are so much more enjoyable. I would greatly simplify the *Aeneid* too. For instance, I would not go on about the fact that Aeneas is an exile, a victim of persecution, and thus someone who would not wish to kill unless fate in some way forced him to. I would focus attention exclusively on the moment when Aeneas carries Dido into the cave and the Nymphs are heard shrieking.

If even this method of abridgement does not render the classics sufficiently interesting, they can as a last resort be reduced to a line or two. Let's try a few examples:

The Odyssey: If Odysseus doesn't come home soon, they'll pinch his wife.

The Iliad (in dialogue form):
'You know Achilles...'
'What about him?'
'He's really pissed off.'

Oedipus Rex: The man who finally solved the Riddle of the Sphinx or (in dialogue form):
'Oedipus went to bed with his mum.'
'Aha!'

Ovid, *Metamorphoses* (talking to the plants, as one does):
'My dear, how you've changed!'

4

Belated Invocation

Dear Superior,[1] who art in heaven, will I ever bring this book
on the classics in the age of buzz to an end? Now that I have
almost reached the halfway point, I find myself depressed.
And you're not giving me any help. I should have called upon
you at the start, I know, as poets have customarily called
upon the Muses and other patrons. But I forgot. And I have
frequently assumed a sarcastic, even irreverent, tone, especially when I wrote about quoting the classics and reducing
them to just a few words. And now I sense that you want to
punish me by shutting off the waters of the Castalian spring.
Without that water, how can I continue?

Forgive me, Superior. Accept the story that follows, which
resembles an allegory, a nobler and more refined form. It is
still about the classics or, more precisely, the classical canon.
This is a much more serious problem than those I have dealt
with so far; yet sooner or later we have to face it. In the midst
of the daily confusion of our lives, how do we decide which are
the really important classics and which are not? Above all,
who decides? Someone needs to tell us which are the genuine
classics, as opposed to the large number of works that are
simply ancient, but possess very little of 'the classical'. Here,
then, is my story.

5

Time and the Canon

The canon and personal time

Every September we used to go up to Casale Marittimo. We had a house there and a small piece of land where Sincero kept a small dog by the name of Buba with a tendency to bite.

Casale is a medieval town built of yellow stone, a cluster of houses which look almost as if they have spilled out of the Castle. As for Sincero, he was an ex-coalminer, construction worker and farmer, who in those days used to look after our smallholding. Most of his days were spent defending the muscovy ducks from the ambushes of Buba, who longed to sink his fangs into them. He succeeded once, and there was a terrible mess. Buba was without doubt the most repulsive dog I've ever known. Sincero, on the other hand, was a good friend. But the person I liked to visit most when we were at Casale was Renzo the barber.

Renzo was one of the last barbers in Italy to play the guitar. There was a time when guitar-playing barbers were a glorious and numerous race. Alas, their little shops, once filled with the aroma of almond soap, have now been supplanted by unisex hair salons (where the sexes in fact continue to do their best to ignore one another). Guitar-playing barbers even predate the era of nude calendars and men's magazines. A barber who played the guitar was usually a virtuous clean-living man, as indeed was Renzo. He kept his guitar hanging on a nail in the wall, and worked for the most part only on Saturday and Sunday. He opened the shop the rest of the week, but only in order to play the guitar and from time to time shave the beards of the idle rich. When a customer turned up he would hang up his guitar for half an hour, but after he had finished he would always start playing again.

I too played the guitar, though not very well. My teachers up to this point had been pretty low grade. The latest was a man called Pasquinelli, a short-sighted fat man who lived in Livorno. I invariably found him seated at table with his family – his mother-in-law, wife and daughter – all as fat as he was. I didn't like him because his fingers smeared mortadella grease on the pages of my Carulli primer. This was the aristocratic school of music from which I came to Renzo's workplace. When I arrived I always had to beg Renzo to take down his guitar from the wall. Then he would bring out his mandolin, which he had just happened to restring the day before because the last time he had played it was a year ago, when I was last around. He used to claim that the only instrument he played regularly those days was the harmonium in church, and then only because the parish priest asked him to. He had a tendency to appear more pious than he really was.

Back then, the people of Casale had a charming habit of never betraying one another: they would pretend to be unaware of something while at the same time letting you know that they knew. The local saying that best summarises this is 'I have the impression – but I may be wrong' ('*Mi pareva e un mi pareva*'), which initiated every conversation in the main square of the town. Renzo was like this too. He waited for me, he knew I would come and that we would play together (that was why he had strung his mandolin), but he had to pretend that this was a coincidence, and that nowadays he only played the harmonium. I never once heard Renzo play the harmonium, but in any case I much preferred to hear him play the piece called *Silvestri's Serenade* on the mandolin, because that is when I got to accompany him on my guitar.

The part I played in this recital was minimal, owing to my limited talents. But I was deeply moved by the experience of changing from the D minor chord I had been strumming on the first four strings to the 'explosion' of a G minor chord that Renzo had taught me. I had to press down hard on the G of the sixth string. 'Bravo!' he said with his eyes. 'Well done.' The lilt of the mandolin went on long after that mutual rush of adrenalin had passed, and I followed the thread of a nostalgic melody that stirred up memories for me of girls I'd left behind at seaside resorts, and for Renzo of I know not what.

It was at the end of one of our many performances of the *Serenade* that Renzo told me about General Cerboneschi. An ageing soldier then in retirement, and a native of Casale like my father, Cerboneschi had returned to his home town and developed an unusual interest in classical music. He passed his days beside his record player and was so obsessed with looking for records and playing them that it eventually became difficult to converse with him. He lived within the Castle precinct. An old general who loved music so much that he had gone mad, who understood the intricacies of Beethoven and the poetry of Chopin! And living right here in Casale – I would never have expected to find such a person living in my home town! Perhaps he knew about the guitar too – maybe we could get together and discuss Sor or the pavanes of Luis Milán.[1] And it was thus, humming the Serenade to myself and slightly flexing my elbow each time my mental melody reached the mystical 'explosion' of G minor, that I climbed up the alleyways of the Castle. I had decided to look for the house where General Cerboneschi lived.

Finding it was no problem. After only a few steps I

distinctly heard Schubert's *Unfinished Symphony* drifting
from the windows of one of the houses above me, more or less
the highest house on the hill. I found the entranceway, rang
the doorbell and set off up the stairs. Cerboneschi came in
person to let me in, as Schubert's notes spilled out onto the
landing. The reason for my visit must have seemed rather
vague to the general, who, despite the obvious enthusiasm I
displayed for the *Unfinished Symphony*, remained stubbornly
on his feet and on the defensive. He said, in effect, that his
passion for classical music was insatiable. Throughout his
life, from parade inspections to flag raisings, he had dreamed
of listening to it but never had the chance to do so. Now he
had retired he could finally realise his dream. But he was still
way behind with a long way to go.

When we finally began to discuss the guitar, a subject I
introduced by appealing to my friendship with Renzo, I found
myself deeply, if predictably, disappointed by his response. He
showed little interest in my beloved instrument, and the
names of Sor and Villa-Lobos meant absolutely nothing to
him.[2] His exact words to me were: 'Music for the guitar is a
lesser form, and I have no interest in it. First, I must get to
know Bach, Beethoven, Brahms and many others.' Then he
added: 'I don't have much time to do it.' That said, he turned
his eyes to the record-player and I understood that he wanted
to return to Schubert. I said goodbye, and the general closed
the door.

I remembered the general when, many years later, I visited
Claude Lévi-Strauss at the Collège de France. I had been
studying his books for some time and was on the verge of
finishing a long study of Roman family relationships, almost
entirely inspired by his *Structures élémentaires de la parenté*.
Like many of my generation, I had (and still have) a sort of
veneration for Lévi-Strauss. I had sent him offprints of my
articles, to which he had responded with courteous letters

from which, however, it was apparent that he had such difficulty with Italian that he could not have made much of what I had written, for example, on the maternal uncle in Rome. But what difference did that make? Lévi-Strauss was Lévi-Strauss. I could not conclude my research on family relationships without going to see him in person. It was to be a rite of passage – an affirmation or even a rejection – who could say? I got up from the park bench in Marcelin Berthelot square, where I had been sitting with notebook in hand, and entered the building that housed the Collège.

Much like General Cerboneschi, Lévi-Strauss had a very small office at the top of a steep flight of stairs. The door stood directly opposite the stairway. I entered. He was seated at the desk, with the same small face behind glasses that I had come to know from photographs and his rare appearances for public lectures. I sat down. My discoveries on the 'pattern of affections' in Rome did not seem to make much of an impression on him. He responded by citing some cautious parallels drawn from the traditions of the French countryside, and then added that he was now devoting his efforts to a thorough analysis of Japanese culture, which took up all the time he had at his disposal. We agreed that I would send him a copy of the book as soon as it was published. Naturally, we both passed over in silence the fact that, as usual, the book would appear in my accursed Italian. The conversation was over. I shook his hand and went down the stairs of the Collège humming Silvestri's *Serenade*.

Each person lives his or her own life, and it runs on a tape that rarely moves at exactly the same speed as that at which others' lives unwind. This is particularly so when the spool has already been spinning for quite some time and the tape is near its end. General Cerboneschi, at the top of the castle steps, had made his own 'canon' of the classics; in his case the musical classics, and he did not have the slightest intention of changing it on the basis of suggestions from a total stranger. Even Lévi-Strauss had made a choice of that sort, and as a result was entirely absorbed in reading medieval Japanese novels such as *Genji Monogatari* or *Heike Monogatari*. Despite the combined efforts of critics and scholars, the canon of the classics is produced by the life and time we have at our disposal. A few months after our encounter General Cerboneschi died and the sound of his furious record-player was heard no more. Who knows how far he had reached in the canon?

When I come across an umpteenth article re-evaluating the greatness of Persius or exalting the (well hidden) stylistic talents of Florus,[3] I always have an urge to send the author to the top of some flight of stairs to convince a General Cerboneschi or Claude Lévi-Strauss of his or her personal theories. If the author is fairly young, he or she will almost certainly come back down a bit disappointed, but nonetheless whistling Silvestri's *Serenade*. If the author is no longer young, it is probably best not to attempt the climb.

Freeing Propertius from the Philologists

Have you forgiven me now, Superior? I fear you have not – that you need something more than the story from Casale to placate you. You always did like Casale, though, so perhaps you will be a little less angry than you were before. Superior prefers us always to deal with serious, safe subjects – even those a bit on the boring side, and he cannot bear to see the classics treated so frivolously. And I too am concerned, for I cannot be sure how much more water the Castalian springs will allow me. So I had best go back straight away to the point where I left off – the use of the classics as a source of excitement. We might well ask ourselves what kind of itch we are attempting to scratch when we set about trying to make the classics exciting and pleasurable?

To respond to the question, let us begin with the time Ezra Pound 'had been seen in the shade', comfortably recumbent on Mount Helicon. Nothing wrong with that, you might think, especially for a poet. Except that Propertius' text,[4] from which Pound drew inspiration,[5] goes like this:

> Visus eram molli recumbans Heliconis in umbra
>   Bellerophontei qua fluit umor equi,
> Reges alba tuos et regum facta tuorum
>   Tantum operis, nervis hiscere posse meis

In translation this reads; 'I dreamed that lying in the soft shade of Helicon where flows the fountain of Bellerophon's horse, I possessed the power to proclaim to my lyre's accompaniment Alba's kings and their deeds, a mighty task.' Propertius was referring to a dream he had had on the mountain of the Muses, according to the poetic model established by 'father Ennius' (another serious literary dreamer, especially in the mountains). To describe that oneiric experience, Propertius used a very common deponent verb, *videor* ('I seem', here in the form *visus eram*, translated 'I dreamed'). But Pound translated this 'I had been seen'. What the devil got into him, making a mistake in the translation of a verb as simple as *videor*?

All hell broke loose. Harriet Monroe, editor of the journal *Poetry*, which had first published portions of Pound's *Homage to Sextus Propertius*, received an indignant letter from William Gardner Hale, an elderly Latinist at the University of Chicago. 'Pound is incredibly ignorant of Latin,' Hale wrote, not mincing his words. 'He has of course a perfect right to be, but not if he translates from it. The result of his ignorance is that much of what he makes his author say is unintelligible.'[6] And the unpleasant episode of the verb *videor* was not the only one. In Propertius' original text there also occurred the word *canes* (the second person singular of the future tense of the verb *cano*, 'to sing'),[7] which in Pound's translation had become 'dogs', or to be more precise 'night dogs', for finding the word *nocturnae* in the same line (which in fact referred to something else altogether), Pound had decided to put the two together, mistaking the verb *cano* for the noun *canis*, dog. Moreover, Pound seemed particularly taken by the idea that the verb *rigare* meant not 'to gush out' (of the waters) but 'to be rigid'. Thus, on at least two occasions, he inserted the adjective 'stiff' where there should have been only flowing waters.[8] A particularly startling moment occurred when 'the gardens of the Phaeacians' (*Phaeacas ... silvas*)[9] became 'the forests of Phaeacia'[10] – the fertile orchards (*pomaria*) of Alcinous are supplanted by a wild forest. Propertius is entirely to blame for calling the gardens *silvae*. And Pound was concerned to add his own pair of epithets to those startling 'forests of Phaeacia' – 'Ionian' and 'luxurious'. I assume he was confusing the Phaeacia of Alcinous with the colony (Ionian, and as such perhaps also luxurious) of Phocaea.[11]

But to continue to insist on the faults of Pound as a Latinist would be a waste of time. Hale was right, no doubt, but he was also small-minded. He saw Pound's errors, but he seemed absolutely incapable of appreciating the outstanding poetic merits that the *Homage to Sextus Propertius* was able to summon in its own defence. Hale may have been a well trained classicist, but he was distinctly hostile to literature. Pound was certainly overdoing it when he described Hale as an 'old brute' and an 'ass',[12] but he scored a point when he raised his aim from the particular criticisms he had received to a more general target: 'If I were a professor of Latin in Chicago I should probably have to resign on divulging the fact that Propertius occasionally *copulavit*, i.e. rogered a woman to whom he was not legally wedded.' Despite the harshness of the language, this affirmation shows that Pound undoubtedly had a powerful instinct for the essence of poetry. And also, if I can put it this way, for the essence of life.

Hale erred when he couched his disagreement with Pound in terms of ignorance. The accusation of having translated from a language he hardly knew would surely not frighten a person who, only four years earlier, had published a collection of 'translations' of Chinese poems entitled *Cathay*. Pound put them together on the basis of notes left by the late Sinologist, Ernest Fenollosa.[13] Scruples concerning philological accuracy were fairly low on Pound's list of priorities. If that was the state of his Latin, what must his Chinese have been like? In reviewing the collection, Ford Madox Ford wrote, 'The [volume] contains renderings of Chinese poems that are a thousand years old – at least I suppose that they are renderings and not part of a mystification by the bard of Idaho – or is it Montana?'[14] One can easily imagine Hale's reaction had he picked up *Cathay* and found a Chinese girl 'lovely ... up in the palace, radiant ... at the window' rendered, in Pound's version, 'within, the mistress, in the midmost of her youth, white, white of face, hesitates, passing the door'. There follow thoughts on the marriage of this girl, which in the original text was arranged with a 'world traveller who had gone away and not returned', while in Pound's translation she turns out to 'have married a sot, who now goes drunkenly out'.[15] Two completely different girls: if one had passed the fabled door of the other, she wouldn't even have stopped to say hello. 'Why should I have anything to do with the wife of an alcoholic?' the wife of the world traveller would say. Fortunately, Hale was a Latinist, not a Sinologist.

Pound's modern Propertius

Let us pick up Propertius once again – the Propertius 'created' by Pound, and as such a poet as poorly trained in his native Latin as he was gifted with a bizarre desire to do things for the fun of it. The real Propertius claimed that fame increases after death, and that, if this were not so, heroes such as Deiphobus, Polydamas and Paris 'would scarcely be known to the ground that covers them' (*vix sua nosset humus*).[16] But that is not enough for Pound: better to say 'their dooryards would scarcely know them'.[17] Later, when we come to the rich 'pillars of Taenarian marble' on which the house of the poet, to his misfortune, does not rest (*quod non Taenariis domus est mihi fulta columnis*),[18] Pound considers it appropriate to amplify the description adding one of those glosses typically found in a grammatical commentary and generally of no help in understanding the text: 'Taenarian columns from / Laconia (associated with Neptune and Cerberus)'.[19] Next, Pound wrestles with a Propertius inflamed by passion; the poet declares that he does not care if death overtakes him (*si certa meos sequerentur funera casus*)[20] as he goes to Tivoli, in the middle of the night, to the house of Cynthia. Pound does not hesitate to play around in his characteristic way with the verb *sequor*, and to squeeze out of the noun *funera* dynamic and unexpected images: 'What if undertakers follow my track ...' Clearly undertakers are always ready to follow a good lead!

However, the real point is that Pound has decided to liberate his author. In his opinion, a reviewer such as Hale – one highly trained in Latin – offers a good example 'of why Latin poets are not read ... of why one would like to deliver poets of philologers'.[21] Responding to another of his critics, Adrian Collins,[22] Pound declared that 'the philologists have so succeeded in stripping the classics of interest that I have already had more than one reader who has asked me, "Who was Propertius?" ' A bitter pill for a philologist to swallow! Pound had in fact thought things through for himself well before he was confronted by the criticisms of his *Homage* put forward by these eminent Latinists. He had written thus to Margaret Anderson in 1917: 'the classics, "ancient and modern", are precisely the acids to gnaw through the thongs and bull-hides with which we are tied by our schoolmasters.'[23] To deliver, to gnaw through. If you agree with Pound, Propertius must be rewritten in order to free him from the academics. But can this be the case?

We can agree that scholars have often conspired to make the classics pretty unattractive – a vice that can be traced back to antiquity, long before Pound probably suspected. For example, Paulus Orosius, a Latin scholar of the fifth century AD who wrote a universal history that moves fairly rapidly from the Creation to his own times, took it for granted that, at school, you would have had to absorb a number of tedious facts about Aeneas' arrival in Latium:[24]

> Furthermore, in the intervening years, came Aeneas' arrival
>   in Italy from Troy
> as a fugitive, the strife he aroused, the wars he stirred up over
>   a period of
> three years, the many peoples he involved in hatred and
>   afflicted with
> destruction, all these have been branded (*inustum*) on our
>   minds by the
> instruction of the elementary school.

Those elementary school lessons may have been useful to Orosius when it came to compiling his chapter on Italy, but his tone in recalling them is far from fond. The very way he describes the lessons as being branded with fire (*inustum*) into the memory makes me suspect that Hale would have seemed an aesthete devoted to the worship of literature by comparison with Orosius' teacher. And even longer ago, at the very dawn of Latin literature, seven centuries before Orosius studied the *Aeneid*, Livius Andronicus was translating the *Odyssey* and explaining it to his students. Fortunately we have reason to believe that his lectures on Homer were more interesting than those that Orosius attended on Vergil.

The classics have always been around and, even more significantly, they've never been *alone*. There has always been someone there explaining how we should interpret them. The classics have taken the form of papyrus scrolls, embellished by written notes and commentaries; then parchment codices, with scholia in the margin; then printed books, with notes at the foot of the page. For several centuries they have occupied shelves shared with lexicons, monographs, further commentaries. There are more editions of the classics today than ever before, and no one will ever manage to read them all. However, in an insistent, almost scornful voice they demand to be read: Are you going to come over here and read us or not? Sit down on that bench and read. We know the light's not good, but read on anyway!

Scholars must surely bear much of the blame for this. However, as far as one can tell from his *Homage*, Pound had it in for Propertius himself as well as for the professors. He admired the Latin poet, but only up to a point. You can see this at the point in the poem when Propertius has quarrelled with Cynthia and receives a visit from the slave Lygdamus, who conveys news of Cynthia (*Elegiae* 3.6). From the slave's account, Propertius learns that his beloved is weeping and depressed; she reproaches Propertius for opening his home to a prostitute who has bewitched him. She goes so far as to swear she'll get revenge. So Cynthia still loves him! If it is as you say, Propertius tells Lygdamus, run immediately to Cynthia's house and tell her that I never wanted to deceive her, I was just angry. For the last twelve days I have remained chaste. If you help me make peace with her I'll grant you your freedom. A typical lover's quarrel, in other

72

words, and the usual haste to make up and start again. But
Pound didn't like the ending. Perhaps he found Propertius a
bit too credulous or sentimental. So, once Lygdamus has
finished his account, Pound's Propertius exclaims: 'And you
expect me to believe that after twelve months of discomfort?'
It may be that the discomfort to which Pound's Propertius
refers should be taken in a sexual sense. In any case, even if
Hale were to overcome his horror at the erotic allusion of the
'discomfort', he would focus with glee upon the fact that the
twelve days of the original have become twelve months in
Pound. To me it is far more interesting that Pound's
Propertius, in distinct contrast to the original, has no intention of believing Lygdamus. In Pound's original typescript
the poem had one more verse and ended as follows; '*And* I
said that I'd pay the bill?'[25] Pound's Propertius is not at all
inclined to pass for an idiot. He doesn't believe Cynthia, and
he has even less faith in Lygdamus. Thus he has no intention
of shelling out a single penny from his own pocket. This
fourth section of the *Homage* is entitled 'Difference of
Opinion with Lygdamus'. The difference of opinion was
really with Propertius.

Propertius apparently behaved in a way Pound did not like,
so Pound made him react as he thought fit. Above all,
Propertius *wrote* in a way Pound did not like, so Pound
rewrote him, inserting things not there in the original,
making his language work in an ironic way, and transforming
him into a critic of Augustan magniloquence. Better yet,
Pound made him a poet who, at the right moment, was
capable of refusing to pay out a single coin if someone tried to
take him for a ride. Pound said that he had it in for the
professors; in reality, he had it in for the classics. Basically, he
criticised them for not being modern. One can sympathise.
You sit down to read Propertius – a love poet, a fairly
dissolute one at that, and, most of all, a sophisticated reader

of Alexandrian poetry. You expect to find in his writings some sort of fellow feeling, but you soon realise you are holding in your hands a string of very disciplined elegiac couplets, replete with allusions to mythology and respectful dedications to Augustus and Maecenas. What kind of poet is this?

So Propertius is rewritten – on the pretext not of freeing him from himself, but of freeing him from the professors. The claim is that academics have distorted, devalued and trivialised him until now, but at last someone has come along who will make everyone understand what Propertius was really like: thoroughly modern. The author himself is innocent; the blame falls entirely on the academics. Among their many sins, they constantly remind us, in their footnotes and their stylistic and philological analyses, that the classics are *not* modern but the offspring of a world that is *not* our own and, as such, profoundly *different* from our own. They come from a world where a man who had spent a blissful night with his lover felt the need to express his satisfaction in a variety of arcane mythological references, and having bothered to write a nice introduction to his poem also gave his all in dedicating it with great care to Maecenas. And the academics are concerned to make sure that none of this is forgotten.

When Livius Andronicus translated the *Odyssey* into Latin for the first time in the third century BC, he was extremely careful to keep Homer's 'otherness' alive. To give the Romans an idea of the extent to which Homer's language was archaic, solemn and far removed from the present, he searched for words that were already considered old-fashioned in his own day. He used *puera* instead of *puella*, *dacrimae* for *lacrimae*, and when he had to say 'immediately' he used the obsolete adverb *topper* instead of the normal *cito*. When it came to translating the famous opening of the poem, *Andra moi ennepe Mousa* ('Sing to me of the man, O Muse'), in order to render *ennepe* ('sing'), Andronicus went fishing for the verb

74

insece, which is not only phonetically similar but distantly related to *ennepe*. Andronicus must have been a good scholar. Otherwise, nothing would have prevented him from rewriting the Introduction to the *Odyssey*, putting in some Alexandrian Muses and making dozens of clever references to recondite Hellenistic poets. Andronicus had respect for the classics. He sensed that Homer's work was already something far removed from his own time, and he tried at every turn to emphasise Homer's otherness.

Unfortunately every generation produces academics who declare that they are convinced of the modernity or – even worse – the relevance of the classics. And they try to prove the point through subtle interpretation of texts. If we are lucky, we'll only have to deal with people such as Pound – the sort who rewrite or 'update' the classics by following the literary convention or fashion of the moment. If we are less fortunate, we'll find ourselves in the company of scholars who declare that the classics are modern and relevant simply because the ancients suffered when in love and ate when they were hungry. How human! The fact is that some values are eternal. As Diego says in *Gil Blas de Santillane*, 'my uncle ... is quite master of the ancients ... had it not been for him, we should never have known that in the city of Athens children cried when they were flogged'.[26]

Pound was a likeable hypocrite. His *Homage* is a masterpiece of irony and often of poetry too – but why claim that it liberates Propertius from the likes of Professor Hale? In fact *Homage* can be regarded as freeing Propertius from himself – or indeed as a self-portrait of Pound finally liberated from the weight of the classics. For the classics can weigh us down like a bad dream: it takes a great deal of energy perpetually to confront their *otherness*. They throw up too many questions. Why does Propertius employ so many mythological references simply to speak about his love? Why does Tacitus always feel compelled to invent subtle and unlikely explanations for every act he chronicles? Even the so-called minor classics prove no exception. Consider Rutilius Namatianus, the aristocratic Gaul who in about 417 AD embarked on a long, exhausting journey from Rome to his native land. How could he compose a poem describing his journey without ever once describing the inns or other resting-places along the way? He must have stopped somewhere, yet he never says a word about it.[27] Presumably he did not consider humble *tabernae* (inns) and *deversoria* (lodgings) a worthy subject for poetry. Then there are the mysteries of Greek tragedy: why on earth, for example, does Sophocles entrust such a significant role to a group of elderly Thebans, speaking in a difficult metre, who follow Oedipus around on stage?

We can perhaps begin to understand why there have been people of some integrity who have longed to be liberated not from the academics but from the classics themselves. Lifting their eyes from these troublesome texts, they have sought the bright gleam of a saviour who will declare, once and for all, that the classics are inferior to modernity. In about 1829 Joseph de Berchoux spoke for them all when he begged, 'Who will deliver me from the Greeks and Romans?'[28] He did not pick a fight with the interpreters, but with the classics themselves, and he made a personal issue of it. It takes too much energy to read the classics, and when one has ploughed through them one is still disappointed because they are not modern. So let's liberate ourselves from them once and for all.

But abolishing the classics is not that simple. They are so rooted in our culture that if we cut them away, we risk killing the whole vine, including its youngest branches. And we haven't even considered the problem of *where* to begin to prune. Let's say, following Berchoux, that it's a question of ridding ourselves of all writings in Greek and Latin. In that

5. *Time and the Canon*

case we'll have to face the problem of Dante, whose *Divine Comedy* will make very little sense once we have liberated ourselves from Vergil's *Aeneid*. And if, in order to solve this problem, we decide to cut away Dante too, we risk setting off a reaction that will destroy the whole of literature. Our literary history is a cloth that requires careful handling; we may think we are just trimming away the excess only to find that we have cut the seam. Assume that we want to rid ourselves of Seneca the tragedian: what do we then do with the Elizabethan poets? Why save them and not Seneca, who inspired them?

It is impossible for us to free ourselves from the classics. Even Berchoux was probably aware of this, and his plea was surely an understandable way for him to vent his frustrations. Pound fought the classics with cunning, rewriting Propertius in his own style and thereby satisfying his craving to transform the Roman poet into a disciple of Laforgue. Pound, pioneer of much of the poetry and culture of the twentieth century, is partly responsible for our modern attitude to the classics. I return to the question I posed at the beginning of this chapter: just what sort of itch are we trying to scratch when we set out to make the classics enjoyable and pleasurable? Now we know the answer – the urge to free ourselves from them. Just rewrite them as you would like them to be. And prevent them from being classics.

77

6

The Search for the Classics

The literary detectives

What were classical authors really like? This is another good
subject to tackle, clearly related to the themes we have dealt
with so far. Surely we gain great satisfaction when we succeed
in conveying to someone else what Sophocles or Homer was
'really' like? One thing, however, must be made clear right
from the start: whenever we decide to enter this territory,
sooner or later we have to leave the world of classical texts
and enter that of their *interpretation*. This is a world in which
much is missing, but there are plenty of surprises. And it is
often the texts that are the most surprised of all.

When a text is interpreted, it is usually pushed back behind
the scenes, leaving undisputed control of the stage to the
interpreter. And the interpreter, as soon as he realises that
the text can't hear, automatically considers himself authorised to satisfy an extraordinary number of sudden urges.
Some interpreters have been known to rub their hands with
glee as soon as they are left alone on stage. And they get right
down to interpreting.

For instance, an interpreter can write a whole book
attempting to show that Oedipus was innocent: he didn't
really kill his father or sleep with his mother.[1] So what actually happened? It was all a cunning plot by Creon and
Tiresias. There is no real evidence against Oedipus; he
blinded himself for nothing. As soon as Sophocles has walked

offstage, the critic has a sudden urge to become a scrupulous judge, an investigative reporter, a relative of the condemned – indeed any of those persons who, especially in American films, subject the records of the court to detailed analysis in order to show how flawed were the proceedings that led to the guilty verdict. With a certain amount of envy, we may grant that the interpreter in question gained great satisfaction from his efforts. From time immemorial, Oedipus has been the archetype of the guilty man, the impure person, the corrupting presence. And now his complete innocence has been demonstrated! The only thing left is to prove that it was really Socrates who did it.

Let's call a spade a spade: even among those classical texts that present themselves as serious and austere, there are impostors. In every corner of the library you will find not only the unjustly accused but also braggarts and frauds. And it is the responsibility of the interpreters to put things right. If Oedipus was innocent, what about Ovid? He claimed to have ended up in exile at Tomis on the Black Sea because of an unspecified *carmen* (poem) and an even vaguer *error* (mistake), which had angered Augustus. From Tomis, for eight long years, he bombarded his friends and patrons with elegies which were later collected into books with the not terribly appealing titles *Tristia* (*Sorrows*) and *Epistulae ex Ponto* (*Letters from the Black Sea*). He also claimed to have mastered the local language, Getic, and even to have written a poem in it. (The Romanians are still proud of that phantom poem today, placing it at the forefront of their literary history.) In other words, Ovid kept himself busy at Tomis. He also learnt the strange names of Black Sea fish and incorporated them into a poem entitled *Halieutica*. Above all, he used elegiac couplets to bemoan his fate more loudly that anyone had ever done before. Ovid, you sly dog!

I take no pleasure in describing him thus, but what else can

one say of a man who for almost twenty centuries led the
world to believe that he had passed eight terrible years in
exile, even though he *never left Rome*? Yes, there are interpreters who have no doubts on this score.[2] To start with, the
temperature Ovid reports is wrong: he describes Tomis and
its surroundings as frozen over with ice – a sort of North Pole.
By contrast, the Romanian National Tourist Board assures us
that the climate of the region is identical to that of central
Italy.[3] Science too proves Ovid wrong. Deploring the endless
winter that tormented him throughout his exile, Ovid
describes an occasion when the wine froze in its container;
instead of being poured into cups, it was handed out in
chunks – a most distressing experience for someone of his
Mediterranean background. However, a chemistry professor
has conducted certain experiments on behalf of one interpreter, which proved irrefutably that wine does not freeze in
a bottle until the temperature has descended below −4°F. This
is a temperature that, again according to the Romanian
National Tourist Board, is absolutely never reached in the
region of Tomis.

Our interpreter proceeds with irrefutable logic, just like a
private investigator: I wouldn't be at all surprised to find him
living with his own Dr Watson, and to hear the faint sounds
of a violin occasionally drifting from their window. Except, of
course, that poor Watson is busily freezing wine in bottles at
the great detective's behest. Our interpreter's logic is inex-
orable: if what Ovid says about his exile is suspect, then so is
what he does *not* say. How can it be that to this day we have
found no plausible reason for his exile? If he had really
suffered such a punishment, surely he would have been far
more explicit about the reason for it? The story of *carmen et
error* is not convincing; it simply doesn't hold water.

(Unless, that is, we are to infer that the great conspiracy of
silence concerning the reason for Ovid's exile can be

explained by the fact that he was a vegetarian. This was precisely the theory put forward by Dr Ernest Bonnejoy in his *Le Végétarisme et le régime végétarien rationel: dogmatisme, histoire, pratique* (1891), which argues from the lengthy praise of Pythagoras in the fifteenth book of the *Metamorphoses* that Ovid was himself a Pythagorean and a vegetarian, and that it was his praise of Pythagoras and his open criticism of Augustus' meat-eating that caused his exile.[4])

However, back to our first interpreter. Reticent about the reasons for his exile, Ovid is even more unforthcoming about the details of his journey. His description is extremely vague and confused, and completely inconsistent with the routes marked on maps (which I assume were also supplied by the Romanian National Tourist Board). In the final analysis there can be no doubt: Ovid lied. He was never in exile.

Of course our interpreter is not just a detective following clues or a devotee of home chemistry experiments – he is also a man of the world. And that is why, at the end of his article, he cannot resist asking the question on all our lips: why would Ovid go to all that trouble? What reason could he possibly have for inventing an imaginary exile? This time, however, our interpreter lets us down. He simply argues that the elegiac poets, on the whole, invented fictitious lovers, and that by extension there is nothing odd about Ovid inventing a fictitious exile to go with his declarations of love for a non-existent Corinna. I consider this a weak argument: our interpreter ought to think again. If everyone who wrote about imaginary lovers also endured imaginary exile the world would become one vast virtual diaspora. Moreover Ovid had a career. He had already written nothing less than the *Metamorphoses*, and he was in the process of writing the *Fasti*, a work which treated the complex subject of the Roman calendar with great wit and urbanity[5] – surely an indication that things were going well. Why would he invent an exile to which he had not been condemned, just in order to write the plaintive elegies of the *Tristia*?

Homeric questions

Spiritus ubi vult spirat (the spirit breathes where it will), says St John's Gospel. And so does the spirit of interpretation. From Sophocles to Ovid, and now to Homer. Given the huge importance and cultural influence of the Homeric poems, an interpreter can satisfy all sorts of cravings – by proving, for instance, that Homer was actually from Trapani, a port on the northwestern tip of Sicily. (This works best when the interpreter is also from Trapani.) Homer's birthplace has always been a source of controversy, even in antiquity, and now the city of Trapani can claim that sublime distinction for itself once and for all. It would be the same story if an interpreter were to prove that Homer was from Marsala, as long as that interpreter was from Marsala too. I'd say the greatest satisfaction was to be gained by the mapping of Odysseus' journey, however. Our interpreter has surrounded himself with nautical charts, sextants and tidal statistics for the last thirty-two centuries – a lot of baggage, considering that he will never leave Trapani. And before he can set out, he needs to make his peace with Eratosthenes.

According to Eratosthenes, you can only reconstruct Odysseus' route once you have 'found the cobbler who has sewn up the goatskin of the winds'.[6] But there is no great difficulty in liberating oneself from Eratosthenes. For a start, he was a real pedantic bore: no wonder he wanted to be called 'philologos'. He was not even a scholar of the first rank: he was nicknamed 'Beta' (i.e. second-best) because he came second in every field of scholarship, immediately behind the leading specialist in that field. Eratosthenes was like a cyclist who never succeeds in winning a race – a perpetual runner-up. How could he presume to make light of Homeric geography? Just watch me reconstruct Odysseus' route!

For reasons of space, I will confine my treatment to Sicily. Even within this limited compass, however, there are many exciting avenues of investigation. For instance, Samuel Butler was fairly certain that both Ithaca and Scheria, the island of the Phaeacians, were based on Trapani.[7] And to make the story a bit more interesting (Trapani is a lovely city, but to set everything there, the encounter with Nausicaa *and* the return home to Penelope ...) Butler also conjectured that the *Odyssey* was written by a woman. This was not a new theory: Richard Bentley had already noted the 'feminine' character of the *Odyssey* compared to the *Iliad*, a poem he considered more 'masculine'. 'The *Ilias*,' wrote the great philologist, 'he made for the men, and the *Odysseïs* for the other sex.'[8] A more direct predecessor to Butler, however, was an ancient writer, Ptolemaeus Chennos, according to whom a woman by the (wholly transparent) name of 'Phantasia', daughter of Nikarchus from the city of Memphis, had written both the *Iliad* and the *Odyssey* and deposited her manuscripts in the temple of Hephaestus in Memphis. When the poet Homer reached Memphis, he made them give him these precious texts and, inspired by them, put together his own poems.[9] In other words, Homer copied everything.

At times life really is stranger than fiction. For it seems that, in March 1901, Butler was on a ferry to Calais when he met a stranger who told him the story of Phantasia. The source the stranger cited, however, was Eustathius' commentary on the *Odyssey*.[10] Butler decided to head for Sicily, but he was already very ill and it would not be long before death caught up with him. However, he found the time and strength to go to the Collegio Romano in Rome in order to verify the accuracy of this information. He tracked down the passage in the library, but was not particularly taken with the idea of Phantasia as the author of the Homeric poems, considering the story 'no more than an interesting corruption of the truth'.[11] Butler was convinced that the author of the *Odyssey* had another name – Nausicaa, that most beautiful princess, who was obviously from Trapani too.[12] Let's face it, Trapani is very appealing as a setting for the *Odyssey*. Later on, Butler's idea so intrigued Robert Graves that Graves decided to base a novel on it – as such a theme deserves. At last we find ourselves face to face with a flesh-and-blood Nausicaa who moves and speaks against the background of an enchanted Mediterranean. The author of the *Odyssey* is forever an exotic and beautiful princess, whom we find almost immediately besieged by dozens of suitors, just like her 'character' Penelope. The discovery of her exceptional poetic talent occurs in Eumaeus' hut, on a memorable night when fleas keep them both awake. And the whole novel, as you might guess, is set in the vicinity of Trapani.[13]

At around the same time as Graves published his novel, Professor Lewis Greville Pocock revived Butler's thesis and backed it up with further learned arguments, going so far as to rate it 'the most important discovery in the history of Homeric criticism'.[14] Pocock corrected Butler on only one point: according to him the *Odyssey* was written by a man, not a woman – but he did come from Trapani.

The debate about Homer's sex has not yet been finally settled. Recently, Louis Paret gave new impetus to the female hypothesis when he published a monograph with the daring title *L'Odyssée d'Homéra*.[15] Too bad that the action of the story has been moved from Trapani to Ischia – we liked the idea that Homer, man or woman, was from Trapani. Needless to say, Colonel Vincenzo Barrabini, born in Trapani, was a dedicated supporter of Butler's theories. In order to avoid any misunderstanding he entitled his book *L'Odissea rivelata*

(The Odyssey Revealed). [16] And the revelation was greeted by five laudatory columns in the local newspaper. [17]

So it is difficult to imagine how the people of Trapani reacted when in 1974 the Gulf of Squillace on the coast of Calabria was renamed 'The Nausicaan Riviera', complete with a stone to mark the exact spot where Odysseus, wretched shipwrecked sailor all covered with brine, first encountered the beautiful Phaeacian princess. How can this be? Wasn't Nausicaa from Trapani? And wasn't Scheria near Trapani? I can only hope that the people of Trapani never got to hear about it. But if they did, and if they wanted to reclaim their rights to the *Odyssey* from Squillace, they would have had a hard time. The interpreters who fixed the location of Scheria in Calabria were two German brothers, Hans-Helmut and Arnim Wolf. [18] You don't take Germans lightly, especially when they share the same family name as the modern founder of Homeric criticism. The brothers Wolf are passionate devotees of anemometers, portulans and nautical charts, but don't think for an instant that these are your typical ivory-tower scholars, reconstructing the world without ever leaving their desks. One of the brothers is actually a scientist – an engineer. However he cannot flatter himself that he is unique. Studies of Homeric geography have some rather peculiar characteristics: just as they are partial to Trapani and the surrounding area, they are also popular, oddly enough, with engineers.

Such was the profession of Aristide Vucetič, a Yugoslavian who died in 1975 at the age of ninety. Vucetič spent a good part of his long life measuring the Adriatic coast in search of the famous cobbler who sewed the goatskin of the winds. His conclusions, set forth in 9,000 pages still in typescript, are rather disturbing: the entire voyage of Odysseus and his men must have taken place along the Croatian coast between Hvar and Dubrovnik – all, that is, except the descent into the underworld, for the entrance to Hades is located on the shore-line of the Po Valley. (Parenthetically, I don't find that part of the shoreline particularly gloomy; at most it is just a bit more polluted than the opposite coast.) Vucetič pinpointed the Cave of Polyphemos on Hvar, even identifying the remains of Odysseus' companions who were devoured by the monster. Even the numbers add up: when he told the awful tale to Alcinous, Odysseus specified that Polyphemos ate six of his companions, and (wouldn't you know it) archaeologists have found the scattered bones of exactly six human beings in the cave of Hvar! It is a pity that Odysseus actually says that Polyphemos, in his greed, 'left nothing behind, neither entrails, nor flesh, nor marrowy bones'.[19] But then Odysseus may have been mistaken: he had a lot on his mind at the time and the odd bone can always be missed.[20]

What is the weather like in Dubrovnik? We know that it rains a lot in Holland, especially in November. And this fact, believe it or not, has very recently been put forward as having momentous consequences for the interpretation of the Homeric poems. The story (the last of the amazing tales to be told in this chapter) goes as follows. A young student by the name of Iman Wilkens is translating the *Iliad* from the original Greek (or to put it in his own words, he has 'the dubious privilege' of doing so) when, lo and behold, he comes across a passage that describes the rain on the plain of Troy. The adjective used by Homer to describe the rain was *athesphatos*, which the young student translates at 'never-ending'. Personally I would prefer the translation 'dreadful' or even 'catastrophic', but that doesn't matter. Young Wilkens looks out of his window and notices that it rains cats and dogs in Holland too in November. And he has a flash of insight. Are you ready to learn that the Trojan War did not take place in Anatolia, as has always been assumed, but in northern Europe?

6. The Search for the Classics

From that rainy day, after some years, was eventually born a book with the evocative title, *Where Troy Once Stood*.[21] It advances a revolutionary thesis, namely that the Homeric poems describe not a Mediterranean world but an Atlantic one. The evidence offered in support of the thesis is essentially as follows: in the *Iliad* it rains a lot, just as it does in Holland; foods such as oysters that are typical of the Atlantic are mentioned (although there are oysters in the Mediterranean they are smaller, really nothing much in comparison); and above all, in one of Homer's similes waters are described as bursting through dykes just as they do in the Low Countries. Other Homeric similes provide essential fodder for Wilkens' thesis. For instance, there are similes that involve calves knocking down fences to reach their mothers, implying that the fences were made of wood. But where, other than in northern Europe, are there wooden fences? In Greece or Anatolia they would have been made of stone. All these arguments are clearly debatable, but they certainly take one by surprise. The reader may be curious to know where Wilkens actually located Troy. That is easily told: the bloody war, tragic graveyard of young heroes, took place entirely in England – to be precise, in Cambridge. The Hellespont therefore corresponds to the English Channel and the North Sea, while Scotland shelters Phrygia and Paphlagonia, and so on. When we turn to the Greek heroes, they were Achaeans gathered from the four corners of the ocean. There are Spaniards, Dutch, Germans, French ... all come together to lay siege to Cambridge.

Moving swiftly on to the *Odyssey*, here too Wilkens presents a dramatic reworking of the tradition. If there must be an ocean setting, then let it be a *proper* ocean. Thus Odysseus in fact sailed as far as the Azores, then on to the Antilles, and he disembarked in Havana, for the Laestrygonians lived in Cuba. Circe, on the other had, lived in

Holland, while the Phaeacians had settled in the Canary Islands. This time Trapani is really up against it: this is a tough nut to crack – even tougher then the Nausicaan Riviera of Squillace. After all his wanderings Odysseus finally returns home to his faithful wife Penelope and his beloved son Telemachos – at Cadiz.

As far as Homer's birthplace goes, you may be pleased to hear that the greatest of all poets wasn't Greek. That would explain why the poems often gives the impression of having been translated from another language, and it would provide a plausible explanation as to why hexameter is so poorly adapted to Homeric dialect. In fact, Homer was Dutch, from the island of Nieuw, which is now part of a larger island called Walcheren. To be precise, Homer 'was born and died a stone's throw from Middleburg Town Hall'.[22] This is part of a caption in Wilkens' book, above which is a photograph of a majestic Gothic building bristling with statues and spires, against a background of maritime clouds. If you look closely, you can see a man in an overcoat carrying two hefty suitcases as he slips around a corner. Homer? From the clothing of the women on bicycles and the heavy horse-drawn carts it looks as if we are around the year 1930.

Chez Propertius

The engineer Vucetič inspires both respect and sadness. He makes you think of a time when it was still possible to meet people on the coast near Dubrovnik who gave up their time to search for the cobbler who sewed the goatskin of the winds. Any sort of *sfizio* or impulse, even the most absurd, is obviously better than war. An impulse is basically harmless. Sometimes it *can* harm texts, despite their rather thick skins, but it rarely harms people. I realise, however, that while I was discussing Vucetič and his sensational discoveries in the cave of Hvar, I unconsciously slipped from the interpretation of classical texts to the interpretation of physical remains. From philology, we have entered the realm of archaeology. This is significant. For worshippers of the *sfizio*, archaeology can be a lot of fun.

Let me try to make a comparison. If a philologist sits down to analyse the story of Romulus and Remus, great satisfaction can be gained from demonstrating that the story is a fiction put together by Roman annalists in imitation of Greek myths; or that it can be traced back to the time of the Indo-Europeans and is very similar to the tale of the Hindu god of fire, Agni, who got drunk on sacred soma and fell asleep under a baobab (a tale that makes no mention of twins or of the founding of a city; but why focus on superficial differences?); or, perhaps, that it is a fertility myth in which the twins correspond to two testicles. With archaeology, however, you can go much further. After detailed investigations, laborious excavations, struggles with local and even national government, the archaeologist can satisfy her urge to pinpoint the exact spot where Romulus slit his brother's throat. 'Now that I look more closely', says the journalist called in to cover the excavation, 'that mark *does* look like a bloodstain, doesn't it?'

As an archaeologist, it is essential that you invite journalists to the site of your discovery. Otherwise, the event will not be *consumed*. Indeed there were journalists present when I was shown round no less a place than the house of Propertius in Assisi. I was deeply moved. I thought of Cynthia, of a youthful Propertius reading Hellenistic poetry by lamplight, and of course, of Ezra Pound. We were ushered into a Roman cryptoporticus located under the church of Santa Maria Maggiore, where the remains of a house attributed by the experts to the age of Augustus are preserved. There were mosaics, fragments of mythological paintings on the walls

89

and epigrams written in Greek. But a Latin inscription stood out from the rest, for it seemed to indicate that someone, probably around AD 367 (though the names of the consuls were incomplete), had come to 'kiss(?) the *domus* Musae'. The day, however, was clear: February 22.

So, on that February 22, someone had come to visit the 'house of poetry', literally designated 'the house of the Muse'. Of course, Musa could easily be a surname, and the crypto-porticus would then merely belong to the house of someone called Musa. But let's not split hairs. What house in Assisi, other than that of Propertius, would be called 'the house of the Muse'? So the cult of the poet had survived in his birth-place, and the city had done well to sponsor a solemn commemoration of the bimillennium of his birth. In fact it was the least they could do. Today, we moderns no longer have just a book of elegies; we have a house in which to put them. Above all, the city of Assisi was able, once and for all, to claim for itself the considerable merit of having been the birthplace of the most famous of the Latin elegists. So much the worse for the surrounding villages that had tried to claim him as one of their own. Any doubts, any alternative hypotheses following the decipherment of the inscriptions – these are matters for specialists.[23] They do not affect the momentous nature of the discovery itself.

There is nothing quite as exciting as this kind of archaeo-logical discovery. There are moments when history becomes suddenly tangible and thrilling, touching those who study the past with a startling immediacy. To this kind of historico-archaeological *sfizio*, the following inscription might be affixed: '... and you too will be able to say that you were there!' These fateful words concluded each episode of an old American television serial. The programme had a title to match and was based on the following simple principle: an historical event such as the battle of Philippi was dramatised, and every now and then a reporter was sent into the anti-Caesarian camp to interview Brutus. Despite Brutus' proverbial reserve, the reporter would find him terribly agitated. He would have had a dream in which Caesar kept repeating 'We'll meet again at Philippi!' Once Napoleon put in an appearance near Waterloo. It was raining and foggy, and the great man must have had his customary stomach-ache since he kept his hand firmly inside his coat. 'Your majesty, do you really think that Wellington's troops ...?' Napoleon responded at length with very complex tactical strategies. Then a duty offer arrived, gasping for breath, to summon him, and the two vanished over a small bridge.

The archaeology of the *sfizio* thus 'enters' history, putting us in direct contact with the blood of Remus or the place where Propertius spent his adolescence. But it does not have to involve events or literary personalities of great importance: the range of possibilities is infinite as long as you have a bit of imagination and a love of minutiae and the commonplace. For instance, I have heard of a schoolteacher, an upright citizen, who developed the following theory: that most of the Etruscan inscriptions that survive describe different varieties of wine that were in circulation in antiquity. He almost always succeeded in establishing some sort of link between the mysterious letters he was trying to decipher and the obscure names of wines that he found in ancient authors. However, there were times when the Etruscan text positively rebelled against any possible link with the name of a wine. In such cases, the teacher printed, below the text of any inscription he had failed to decipher, the following words: 'Unknown wine.'

Monumental enticements

It has to be acknowledged that ancient monuments, much like classical texts, are very unfamiliar objects. In order to interpret a monument you almost always have to assume its extreme remoteness and complexity, and at times not even years of study suffice to bridge the gap. Even our most basic action when faced with a monument, just looking directly at it, can turn out to be entirely misleading. Often the significance of a monument does not lie within itself but in its surroundings, in the complex topographical or stratigraphical context which only an archaeologist can interpret.[24] In other words, the monument is a weighty object in every sense of the word, and one has the impression that many people would really like to 'free themselves' from it, just as Berchoux managed to free himself from the Greeks and Romans. One feels this particularly on guided tours of monuments or museums which, dominated by the learned disquisitions of young officials who pay more attention to scientific data than to amusing anecdotes, almost always turn out to be boring. So you need to deal with the monument as soon as possible. It has to be worked over, unveiled, brought up to date, in order to make it resound as an event of momentous consequence. And that way its thrilling potential can be disclosed to the greatest number of consumers.

In order to make a monument thrilling it is not always necessary, for example, to pinpoint the exact spot where Caesar fell to the ground under the repeated blows of the conspirators. There are more subtle ways to achieve your purpose. However, it is also true that these alternatives, which at first sight may seem simply innocuous and of wide popular appeal, actually turn out to be more damaging to the monuments than any other form of presentation. For instance, you can organise rock concerts inside monuments (the sort that Minister Ronchey justifiably tried to ban[25]), and you can erect within them giant Expos made of tin cans and cardboard boxes. From this perspective Italy seems a nation bristling with monumental impulses that we would do well to gratify as soon as possible. The discerning *sfizio*-hunter appreciates that monuments are much bigger game than, say, Homer's *Odyssey*. The reason for this is in a way theoretical. It is the very semiotic substance of the monument that is much more potent than any classical text.

The text, after all, is almost invariably a copy; it refers us to an intangible lost original. Where is the original copy of the *Aeneid*? No one knows. We possess only manuscript copies written from the fourth century onwards, and in this case we are lucky, for the works of other ancient authors have come down to us far less directly. In the case of the *Odyssey*, for example, we now believe that Homer never really existed, and that the text derives from a compilation of oral performances recorded over time with the assistance of writing. In other words, not only do we not possess the first written copy of the text we call 'The Odyssey', but even if we did we would still not be satisfied, for that first written copy would still be far removed from what we really want – a recording of a radio broadcast of successive oral performances of the poem before it was ever written down.

The Baths of Caracalla, by contrast, are still standing, and they are original. The Baths refer only to themselves; the monument comprises in every respect 'a sign of its own origins'.[26] To put it less technically, if you lean against a wall of the Baths, you can be certain you're leaning against the same wall once worked on by Roman architects and builders. The same can be said of the Arena in Verona, the Colosseum in Rome, and all other ancient monuments. That may explain why, a few years ago, unknown persons entered the archaeological park at Piedigrotta and emptied a rubbish bin over the famous tomb of Vergil that is located there.[27] Another impulse gratified.

How times have changed! In the second century AD, Silius Italicus, an epic poet who imitated Vergil slavishly in his

93

work, went to the tomb of the divine poet annually, not to throw rubbish on it but to celebrate Vergil's birthday as a loyal devotee. In fact Silius had actually bought the tomb in order to have it to himself.[28] One might say that he was somewhat obsessed with it. Once, for instance, when he had to give a brief description of the poet Ennius (who appears in Silius' poems not as a poet but as a brave centurion), he did so in terms clearly reminiscent of Vergil's famous funerary epigram: *Mantua me genuit, Calabri rapuere, tenet nunc Parthenope* ('Mantua bore me, Calabria took me, now Naples holds me').[29] For a centurion who was meant to be alive at the time, this might have seemed a bad omen. But since the epitaph was carved on Vergil's tomb and Silius read it over and over again during his private worship of the master, he began to see it everywhere. Sometimes great poets actually become literary monuments – and that holds beyond the metaphor. There is no doubt that when it came to Vergil's tomb, Silius was far more reverent than those who threw rubbish on it. But I suspect that he managed to satisfy a pretty monumental impulse of his own. How else can one describe the satisfaction of actually owning the tomb of one's personal literary hero?

Raiders of the Lost Ark

In recent years we have so developed the art of archaeological impulse and gratification that we now have a legendary figure as its founding hero. As has always happened in the past, once a given social phenomenon takes on a significant role in society, that society ends up assigning it a hero with his own origin myths. Prometheus discovered fire, evil came from Pandora's box, and the sudden interest in archaeology produced Indiana Jones – who, as we know, satisfies an enormous variety of sudden urges.[30] Most recently we learned that he was doing so even as a child, in the company of young Austro-Hungarian princesses and Chinese conspirators. In any case, once Indiana reached adulthood he became the absolute embodiment of the archaeological impulse. When we meet him at the beginning of the first film, he seems a typical professor condemned to spend his life teaching archaeology to rather dense students at an American university. But it isn't long before he's inside a pyramid, clasping a beautiful women over a pit crawling with serpents.

Indiana has discovered a truly original way to free himself from the classics. He has decided that the world of the past, in itself tranquil and silent, can be suddenly transformed by the breathtaking pace of an action film. It takes genuine talent to conceive such a thing. 'Now where is the sound of those ancient peoples ...?', Giacomo Leopardi used to ask himself.[31] Today we have the answer to that question: it is reverberating in the gunshots of Indiana Jones – or, better still, those of his pursuers. Archaeological ruins have recently become some of the noisiest, most crowded places on earth.

The secret of this sort of archaeological adventure is a storyline as simple as it is profound. In the world of Indiana Jones, the archaeologist's investigations always coincide with the reconstruction of a mysterious event or the unmasking of a villain. Thus a veneer of mystery and glamour is laid over something that has always encompassed elements of the detective story – the very nature of archaeological research being to reconstruct the past out of the fragments that remain to us. It is fortunate that ancient monuments are often located in wild and inaccessible places, so that the search for the Ark, for example, can continually be enriched by all sorts of unexpected events, attacks and dirty tricks. You'd have a hard time fitting all that into the British Library. In this respect, the archaeologist has a clear advantage over any classical philologist: the latter is highly unlikely to be attacked by Bedouins while studying the *scholia* to Pindar. The situation can change suddenly, however, when we deal with the familiar, towering figure of Homer.

With Homer, anything can happen, especially if we throw in Aristotle's *Poetics*. Let me explain. When Aristotle analysed the composition of the Homeric poems in his *Poetics*, he stated a famous principle known to virtually every literary critic: 'Homer constructed his *Odyssey* around a single action (*praxis*), in our sense of the word, and he did the same for the *Iliad*.'[32] No surprise there – it's the usual Aristotelian exaltation of unity. This traditional explanation, however, failed to convince a Turkish philologist, Abdullah Razi. According to him, the Aristotlelian *praxis* or 'action' concealed something much more delicate and secret. He believed that the *praxis* in question was none other than the 'act' *par excellence*: sexual intercourse.[33] In other words, on the basis of discreet clues provided by Aristotle, the *Odyssey* must be interpreted as twenty-four books of protracted coitus. (What would Hale have thought of all this? Surely he would have judged Razi far more dangerous than Pound?)

Razi's hypothesis remained just that for almost 50 years – a hypothesis, though a stimulating one. Until 1940, that is, when excavations directed by Professor Andreou Tikhvin in North Africa led to the discovery of some papyrus scrolls written in the Demotic alphabet, which sensationally confirmed Razi's suspicion. They contained an extremely eroticised *Odyssey*, entirely in line with the Aristotelian precepts so perceptively decoded by Razi. Unfortunately Tikhvin died in the bombing of Benghazi, and at this point we apparently lose all trace of his precious discovery, which had aroused much interest among lovers of things classical. Then the war ended and people began to rediscover their interest in literature and the arts. It was at this time that Colonel Frank Humbert, head of the Allied commission for the recovery of works of art transported to Germany during the war, pointed out that in about 1943 or 1944 a certain Rosenblatt, an officer in the SS, had brought Tikhvin's priceless scrolls to Germany, intending them as a gift for an officer high up in the Gestapo, an aficionado of erotica. Humbert also succeeded in ascertaining that Rosenblatt had had a German version of the new *Odyssey* made, probably because reading it in Demotic tends to inhibit the erotic effect. The news of the trail uncovered by Humbert caused an immediate sensation. Predictably, however, Humbert never managed to get beyond the clues and partial revelations: there was no tangible evidence of the lecherous Nazi, the scrolls, or the German translation of the poem.

But now we find ourselves in 1960, in Argentina. As everyone knows, Argentina was a haven for filthy rich Nazis: we were bound to end up there on the trail of Rosenblatt and the erotic *Odyssey*. A German gentleman by the name of General Gutzler has just died, leaving a considerable estate without heirs. The Argentinian officials assigned to execute his will discover a prominent collection of erotic material (books, photographs, engravings, etc.) together with a German version of the fabled erotic *Odyssey*. Given the contents of this collection, it is immediately made available to Dr Alfred Kinsey. Luckily, however, the diligent Argentinian bureaucrats grasp the significance of the version of the *Odyssey* they've found and arrange for a Spanish translation to be made, assigning the task to a Dr Hernando Pampone. The Spanish version was published by Pampas y Cortiz in Buenos Aires in 1962. Needless to say, in the absence of the original scrolls, classical scholars refused to give any credit to the published text. Not even the study that Dr Pampone explicitly dedicated to the subject[34] succeeded in shaking their determined scepticism. Nonetheless, an English translation of the text, entitled *A Bedside Odyssey*, was finally published some years later.[35] From Homeric Greek to Demotic to German to Spanish to English, it has been a long journey, but we've finally reached our goal: Indiana has at long last brought back the lost Ark.

Let me cite the invocation that opens the poem:

> Come down, O Muse of the white breasts, from the solitary height of your mountains, and through my mouth sing the story of Odysseus, a man expert in every art of love, an alien wanderer through bedrooms, once he had put his strong hands on one or two treasures in the bedrooms of proud Troy ... [36]

The *polytropos*, the man who had wandered far and learned much, has become 'an alien wanderer through bedrooms'. Later, Calypso tried to seduce Odysseus by reminding him of the occasion when Helen, suspecting that the wooden horse was a trick, cunningly approached the immense beast and sweetly called the Greek leaders by name. Fearing that the beautiful Helen would reveal their presence, Odysseus dropped his 'rod' through a hole in the belly of the horse. Awestruck by its great length, Helen went straight to the king of Troy to announce that the horse had been truly blessed by the gods. Could Helen have recognised that rod? The poet asked himself that question, as did Calypso. Perhaps, before Helen was snatched away by Paris, Odysseus had gone hunting on Menelaus' private estates?

The further one goes in one's reading of this unique, protracted, pseudo-Aristotelian *praxis*, the more one becomes convinced that those involved – whether the Turk Razi, the American Humbert, or the Argentinian Pampone – could have saved themselves a great deal of trouble. For in the third century BC, Sotades, a poet and writer of malicious satire from Maronea, had already gone one better with Homer. He took some famous lines from the poems and changed the order of the words to transform solemn hexameter into lustful Ionic metre, and by this simple technique squeezed obscene meanings from the most wholesome Homeric expressions. According to Demetrius, once a Homeric hexameter had passed through Sotades' hands, 'the line seems transformed, as it were, like those who (so the stories go) are changed from men into women'.[37] Strangely, it was those same 'rods' of the Homeric heroes that caught Sotades' attention, just as they had intrigued the author of the erotic *Odyssey*. It must be a case of Jungian archetypes. In the case of the malicious satirist from Maronea, the 'rod' was not lowered from the belly of the horse as in the aforementioned adventure of the lovely Helen. Rather, simply by inverting two words in a celebrated line of the *Iliad*, Sotades managed to create someone shaking his 'rod' in a very threatening manner.[38] Instead of turning to Dr Pampone, the Argentinian officials responsible for Gutzler's legacy should have looked up the Hellenistic poets. But let's not kid ourselves. Sotades was a bizarre and adventurous character, who had the nerve to enrage King Ptolemy II Philadelphus, who was married to his own sister Arsinoe, by insisting that he desist from such Egyptian activities ('push[ing] your goad into an impious hole', as he put it in his characteristically lewd way).[39] For this he was put to death. No one today would think of turning to him to transform the *Odyssey* into an erotic poem. Sotades was a satirist, not a hero, and it seems that nowadays, in order to devote yourself to things classical, you have to be some kind of hero – like Indiana Jones.

The search for secrets

The cultural practice of which Indiana Jones is the mythical founder is much more widespread than I have so far described. Indiana Jones is only one among many 'raiders', and archaeology is not the only branch of knowledge in which it is possible to construct adventure tales and detective stories. In matters of culture, we assume the role of detective with ever greater frequency. Everything is a 'clue'; we look everywhere for fingerprints, tracks, hidden paths – and if those paths turn out to be forked, so much the better. Almost nothing refers simply to itself; everything is immediately taken as a sign of something else that cannot be seen. So, following a trail of clues, we indefatigably work our way back to the so-called 'Other' to which everything else 'refers'. Our whole culture has become deeply mysterious, and it sometimes seems that we have no motive for studying its various manifestations other than to discover secrets or buried treasure. This is sometimes called 'conspiracy theory', sometimes 'intrigue', and it is this subject of intrigue that we will now go on to consider.

Imagine something like a cocoon. Contemplating a literary work or an ancient monument, a scholar is wrapped in a subtle thread: he is 'intrigued', the work 'intrigues' him. That moment of stasis lasts a few minutes at the most, and then he starts to wriggle out, struggling, expending energy: he is 'disentangling himself'. In some ways he resembles the escapologist Houdini, who had himself lowered into the water trussed up like a chicken and, in a matter of seconds, re-emerged triumphant, shaking his freed fists. We are at Hvar, in a cave on the Adriatic coast, with a copy of the *Odyssey* lying open on a small camping table: we are really intrigued by the fact the Homer, when he describes how tall Polyphemus was ...; or perhaps the scene is an Egyptian pyramid with Indiana Jones, trussed up like a chicken of course, suspended over a pit full of serpents. But we might as well be at Cornell University, in a seminar room, with the text of *Oedipus Rex* lying open on the desk. The students are assembled, taut as the strings of a violin. 'What intrigues me

is that Creon, when he quotes the oracle, does not say that ....'
The clock is ticking, the professor must start to 'disentangle'
himself immediately.

In his desperate struggle against the knots that held him,
Houdini put his life on the line. One might well ask why on
earth he took such delight in having himself tied up, placed in
a locked chest and cast into the depths of the Hudson River.
Well, other considerations aside, Houdini knew that if he
succeeded in freeing himself and opening the chest in time, he
would have a chance to breathe again once he had broken the
surface of the Hudson. That's no small reward. But what
reward awaits a scholar who succeeds in getting the better of
the work that has so insidiously intrigued him? Simple: the
'meaning'. When we interpreters find ourselves wrestling
with intriguing works, we have the task of 'getting to the
bottom of things' – we seek some meaning that the text stubbornly refuses to yield.

From time immemorial, people have searched for the
'meaning' of the works they study. We do not attempt to
define what that meaning might be because we are incapable
of doing so. If you discuss semantics with linguists, the most
you will get is an encouraging pat on the back. Yet when
Benedetto Croce defined the poetry of Catullus as 'juvenile',[40]
or when Eliot found that Vergil's poetry showed great signs of
'maturity',[41] it is clear that both critics felt that they had
identified the principal 'meaning' of the works that they had
worked hard to interpret. The search for meaning is an
ancient practice. For instance, Fulgentius Planciades, a
learned African of the fifth century AD, was convinced that
the deepest meaning of Vergil's *Aeneid* was nothing less than
an complete depiction of human life.[42] Good for him; he had
discovered a truly great meaning. When it came to the
Eclogues and *Georgics*, however, Fulgentius refused to deal
with them because he considered them so rich in *mysticae*

101

rationes as to flummox anyone of average intelligence. The precise justification he provided for his decision not to deal with them was as follows: *ne, dum quis laudem quaerit nomine, fragumen repperiat capitis* ('lest someone, seeking praise for his own name, might rather end up rupturing the vessels in his brain').[43] All interpreters seek a meaning in the works they investigate, so long as it does not cause too much of a headache.

In recent times the search for the meaning of literary works has increasingly taken on the guise of a manhunt. The work of a literary critic resembles that of a thriller writer: the meaning must be unmasked and a twist in the tale, a revelation, is *de rigueur*. Among the new rules of hermeneutics, the following stand out: the 'meaning' cannot be the butler or, above all, the detective. Otherwise our plot will carry no weight. As I have mentioned before, Indiana Jones is one of innumerable detectives in our culture, and archaeology is not the only discipline that has served as a setting for thrillers.

As in the American film industry, changes have been taking place recently in the world of textual interpretation. Once we were treated to stories of passion and romance, often accompanied by song. Today, more often than not the defining image in film and TV is that of the unidentified serial killer, sex maniac, homicidal war veteran, face in shadow, pursued by the detective whose task is to unmask and capture this unknown quantity.

In the world of scholastic interpretation, such unmasking can be disconcerting. We have come a long way since Eliot was happy to praise Vergil for his maturity or Croce gently chided Catullus for his childishness. When you chase after a killer, you cannot afford to worry about your manners: you go for the jugular. It is important to engineer a surprise ending. Take the aforementioned study of Sophocles, the one demonstrating that Oedipus was innocent.[44] The first thing to note is how often the critic is rude to the poet. He accuses him of being imprecise, reticent, even dishonest. By contrast, let's see how Fulgentius Planciades behaved. Fulgentius dramatised his interpretation as follows: he asked Vergil questions, and the poet answered them. But Fulgentius portrays himself as timid and respectful, while Vergil is proud and almost scornful. When Vergil addresses his interpreter, he even calls him *homuncule*, 'little man',[45] and he frequently manifests his impatience with the extremely naive questions that are put to him. At one point, Fulgentius asks him how on earth someone as wise as he, who had written a work such as the fourth eclogue, could now and then betray signs of being an Epicurean. And Vergil, with a superior smile, replies, 'If among so many Stoic truths I had not inserted some Epicurean absurdities, I would hardly be a pagan.'[46]

Twists in the tale

Interpreters like Fulgentius respected their authors; today critics have far less respect. What is important is that in every case there should be a final twist, an unexpected denouement, and if in the process someone suffers, too bad. It might be Sophocles, in a tight spot because he lied about Oedipus; indeed it might be anyone, so long as the result is an intriguing situation. For a few days, I made a careful study of the arts pages of a selection of Italian newspapers. It was only a small sample – I make no claim to have conducted an exhaustive investigation into prevailing cultural trends. The experiment could be repeated any time, however, and I doubt that the results would be very different. This is what I learned.

First, I discovered that Don Juan, the greatest of all womanisers, was gay.[47] A Welsh historian, Robert Stradling, recently reconstructed the life of Don Juan de Tarsiss y

Peralta, count of Villamediana and the historical figure who supposedly inspired Tirso de Molina's *Burladór*. The count, an Andalusian gentleman and friend of Philip IV, was killed in mysterious circumstances while out riding in his carriage with a royal page. The Inquisition took up the case, and their investigations established that Tarsiss y Peralta habitually indulged in 'the love that dare not speak its name'. This doesn't come as a complete surprise, since the gentleman in question had previously fallen in love with a young prince of the royal household and made no bones about it. So Don Juan was really a gifted seducer of men: Doña Anna, Doña Elvira, Zerlina, and a thousand and three Spanish women (according to Da Ponte's libretto) were all in pursuit of a man who preferred men. What a paradox. And what a surprise.

Next, it's Forster's turn. We learn that in the original manuscript of *A Passage to India*, the rape of the virgin Adela Quested by the Moslem Dr Aziz actually happened.[48] By the final draft of the novel, however, the evidence for the crime had been suppressed. Perhaps the author himself had good cause to fear such a twist in his narrative. He may have been influenced by the fact that, some fourteen years after the first draft was completed, Hollywood producers began to express interest in the novel, and in those days the movie moguls of California demanded upbeat endings for their films. In other words, like a true criminal, Forster engaged in a cover-up. Forster himself was guilty, not of rape but of homosexuality, and in the famous scene in the Marabar caves he was supposedly concealing the bitter disappointment he felt when his Indian friend, Syed Ross Masood, spurned his amorous advances. It would have been the deeply distressed Adela with whom he identified.

Now let's turn to the *Bounty*. Everyone knows the famous story of the mutiny: it took place in the South Pacific on 28 April 1789, and was caused by the violent irascible personality of the ship's captain, William Bligh. That was what drove the second-in-command, Fletcher Christian, to take command of the ship, forcing Bligh and eighteen crewmen into a lifeboat only twenty-three feet long. But now this has all been overturned.[49] Now we discover that poor Captain Bligh was no sadist; on the contrary, he was a trustworthy officer who had formerly served under the command of Captain Cook. His only fault was that he was sometimes verbally unrestrained. The new biographies of Captain Bligh fill us in on all this, as do the letters that one of the sailors on the *Bounty* regularly sent to his family, which were recently discovered in a library in New South Wales. Everyone has spoken badly of poor Bligh. No one has paid enough attention to Fletcher Christian. As ever, the true culprit is the least likely suspect. The real surprise is that Christian was not a good man. In fact, like a typical lieutenant, he was extremely jealous of his captain, who was a much better sailor. And he was probably driven by the usual contradictory homosexual impulse.

I could go on to the autobiographical material that has made Mussolini so popular in the United States, particularly among Italian-Americans. It was actually written by his mistress, Margherita Sarfatti, who paradoxically was of Jewish ancestry.[50] And then it's Einstein's turn, that insufferable male chauvinist and monster of depravity; or Walt Disney, an FBI spy and alcoholic womaniser who doesn't even deserve the credit for inventing Mickey Mouse, a character he stole from another cartoonist. You can't even trust Snow White: in real life she was a German countess, Margarethe von Waldeck, who had mines on her estates that were worked by children. That's the twist: the dwarves were not dwarves at all but exploited children! Bundled up, bent low with exhaustion and hardship, those poor children looked like dwarves. And while they were working for the pitiless Margarethe (compared to her, the wicked stepmother of the fairytale is a positive Mother Theresa), she fell in love with the young Philip II and died, poisoned in the interests of the state. This story has it all: love, intrigue, cruelty, and great historical events of which we catch only a glimpse as they unfold behind the castle walls. The reconstruction is that of a German historian, Eckhard Sander.[51] I hope he has time to repent before Judgement Day. In any case, if you keep reading you'll be constantly amazed. I should note that the authors of these newspaper articles usually go to great lengths to emphasise their detachment from the matter in hand by citing sources for their various 'discoveries', introducing ironic comments, and using plenty of quotation marks to create distance between text and author. But it is clear that even they will eventually succumb to the element of surprise.

Even in the field of Fine Art it is difficult to be bored. There's a new surprise every day, sometimes more than one. If the painting in the city hall of Siena attributed to Guidoriccio da Fogliano is a nineteenth-century forgery, as has more than once been claimed, what about the Mona Lisa? First she was given a moustache, then her hair was in turn straightened and curled, then she was finally revealed for what she truly represents: a skilfully disguised (Leonardo wasn't just your average artist) pair of buttocks belonging to whichever young boy the artist was lusting after at the time.[52] For it seems that the famous lips of the Mona Lisa, photographed, enlarged and rotated by ninety degrees, clearly represent a pair of buttocks. This, at any rate, is the argument of a genial Canadian scholar from Quebec. The hunt for the young boy has already begun, and sooner or later he is bound to be identified. Yet what makes this discovery, or surprise, so striking is that the meaning of the Mona Lisa, once it has been properly unveiled, is pygic (I apologise for the

Greekism, but I can't think of another suitably scientific term). This is important, for surprising meanings tend towards the phallic as a rule, whatever the work of art. You must have noticed by now that the 'surprises' which I have casually listed in this brief review are almost all sexual. The age of rocket is ever true to itself. In order to have fun with Don Juan, Mona Lisa, even poor Captain Bligh, it's best to entrust the operation to Priapus, or at least to one of his devotees.

And so all of us – literary critics, journalists, historians – have decided to take the ultimate risk: if you're going to bet on the text, you have to go for broke. Elsewhere I tried to compare this type of criticism to the quest for the Holy Grail, whose image flickers before the dismounted knights and their frightened steeds as they wander through the depths of the forest.[53] Only the most worthy can follow its trail, while the sacred chalice, for its part, loves to appear precisely where one would least expect it. And only the initiate senses its presence, while everyone else remains oblivious. Look over there! The Grail! Why haven't the others noticed it? Clearly they are not among the initiates. The fact is that the texts are the first to be unaware of their own 'meaning'. Left to themselves they would remain forever in the dark about the precious mysteries with which they are filled to overflowing. As the Gnostics, passionate students of allegory, used to say, 'the actor ... is accompanied by the lyre; as he sings, he tells of great mysteries, unaware of the meaning of his words.'[54] The text needs help to understand the enormous importance of the meaning which it bears. And because critics are deeply convinced of this, they ensure that every book or article they produce ends by creating a new 'meaning', a complete overturning of previous beliefs – otherwise it will have been an utter waste of time. If you think about it, even deconstruction is all

107

about surprise and revelation. As a result, the text that 'intends to say' what it says, or at least what it was always thought to say, is becoming rarer and rarer. Above all, we love to be *surprised*. But why?

I believe that the cause should once again be sought in the 'vast archive' which has already helped us to understand the phenomena of the anniversary and the calendar. Our civilisation, having stockpiled around two-and-a-half thousand years of texts, has managed to accumulate such a huge amount of information about itself that it is very difficult to decide why we should concentrate on any one thing rather than another. The problem is always the same. Why should we focus on Forster rather than Vergil? Why should we go back to Don Juan rather than Martin Luther? The vast archive is so huge that breeds a sort of paralysis among those who use it. We are all looking for what might be termed a 'good reason' for choosing one subject at the expense of another, or for a subject we can address without boring our audience. And surprise, especially in the guise of sexual revelation, is an excellent reason for picking one subject rather than another. Don Juan surprises me by turning out to be gay when I always thought he was a womaniser – so let's zero in on him. Martin Luther, on the other hand, hasn't changed, doesn't surprise me – so let's leave him alone. The fact is that a surprise, by arousing our curiosity, not only focuses our attention but is fully capable of *capturing* it, even in the vastest archive. A surprise really 'hits' us. The Greeks used the verb *ekplêssomai*, 'I am struck', in order to describe the state of mind that results from being surprised, and the same metaphor is used in many modern languages. Strolling through the vast archive, you are suddenly struck by an interpreter holding a picture of the Mona Lisa in one hand and punching you with the other. The surprise is such that you have no choice but to pay attention.

6. The Search for the Classics

The personification of texts

This technique of delivering a metaphorical punch in the face to the reader requires a certain amount of subtle preparation. It is best employed only when you are absolutely sure that your other hand has a firm grip not only on a text or work of art, but on a famous personality as well. In other words, what counts is being able to transform the object of your investigation into a person. This technique of *prosopopoeia* or personification, which dominates our culture and which we have already discussed in Chapter 2, is essential to the 'surprise' interpretation of literary works, historical events, famous paintings, and so on. Through personification, a complex web of narrated events, style, language, thought, culture etc. – the elements that go together to constitute a 'text' – is compressed to the point that it can actually be contained within the bare outlines of a single character. When I have conflated and boiled down all the various Don Juans/Don Giovannis of literature to one man, Don Juan, a person about whom I can reveal some surprising hidden or paradoxical quality, I can then apply the same 'surprise' technique to the texts of Tirso de Molina or Lorenzo Da Ponte.[55] Without the prior personification of a text or work of art, subsequent surprising revelations are far more difficult to achieve. For example, just try proving that seventeenth-century Castilian prosody had homosexual tendencies – it's a difficult task, and no one would be interested anyway.

Haec autem nacti sumus

I'm afraid that Superior is angry with me again. Perhaps he didn't like the way I compared him to Fulgentius' unpleasant Vergil, but for whatever reason the flow of Castalian water has slowed considerably. Domenico Comparetti described

Fulgentius' Vergil as follows: 'The poet is a scowling know-it-all, gloomy, abrupt and proud – the complete opposite of the gentle, sweet and modest soul expressed in his poetry, which all his biographers have described, and which Dante has so faithfully portrayed.'[56] The problem is that I picture Superior in just the same way, as a scowling know-it-all. Superior would never surprise you, not even to save your life. Even when he's angry, he's never surprising. Perhaps I can calm him down by relating another story about Casale.

My grandfather was a hunter. A long time ago when he was young (a very long time ago, for my grandfather was too old to be drafted when World War I broke out), he used to go on long hunting trips in the local woods. It was nothing like today, when hunters drive right up to pheasants in their cars and empty their shotguns at them. Back then you went alone and on foot. The Maremma was hard going, covered in scrub and thickets, and in those days you did your shooting with discretion. My grandfather told me that skilled hunters would rarely shoot pheasants because they were so easy to hit, and your companions would have made fun of you if you were foolish enough to waste a shot on one. At most, you could fire at a pheasant only if you aimed up from the ground after it was already airborne and hit it squarely in the chest. A pheasant shot in the chest – 'the royal shot' – was a worthy catch. That's how they hunted in the northern Maremma at the end of the nineteenth century. It often happened that they couldn't make it back to Casale by evening, so they'd stop along the way and spend the night with friends or relatives.

Once my grandfather spent the night with a peasant who was a friend of his. The peasant, Garibaldo, was well known as an anarchist and an atheist. The next morning my grandfather and Garibaldo rose early, my grandfather to continue his journey and Garibaldo to go to work. My grandfather happened to see his host make a highly visible sign of the cross. 'Wait a minute,' he said. 'I thought you were an atheist?' And Garibaldo, without the slightest embarrassment, responded, 'Oh, these are things that you just have in you.'

In order to appreciate just how insightful that phrase is, you have only to translate it into Latin, a language notorious for fostering the lapidary aspects of almost any expression. When translated, it reads, *Haec autem nacti sumus*, or perhaps *Haec autem nos nacta sunt*.

Garibaldo was talking about the sign of the cross, but I suspect we could say the same thing about the *Aeneid* or about Vergil himself. The *Aeneid* belongs to that category of items which are just 'there' for us to encounter along the way. Among the many possible definitions of the classics, this one seems the simplest and yet most accurate. The classics are the books we 'just have in us', or which 'just have us', and this has been the case for thousands of years. The classics are intrinsically different from all other books simply because they have been common currency for a very long time.

Definitions of the classics ... according to the Ancients

So the classics have been around for a very long time. They precede all other Western literature. We are bound to encounter them – to bump into them, so to speak – along our way. Maybe that is as good a definition as any.

There have been many fine definitions of 'a classic', despite the difficulty of the task. Later I shall list some recent definitions, but here is the most ancient: a phrase of Aulus Gellius in which (at least according the evidence we have at our disposal) the adjective *classicus* is used for the first time of a writer. Gellius is summarising a long and futile discussion

111

that took place in the house of Cornelius Fronto, tutor to Marcus Aurelius, pedantic scholar and fervent enthusiast for archaic Latin. The discussion was about whether *harena* (sand) could be used in the plural and *quadrigae* (carriage) in the singular. In the end, Fronto himself, realising that the subject they have chosen is not particularly scintillating, sends his guests on their way with these words: 'So go now and inquire, when you chance to have leisure, whether any orator or poet of that earlier band – that is to say, any "classical" or "assiduous" writer, not a "proletarian" – has used *quadriga* or *harenae*.'[57] What an odd definition: what has assiduousness to do with it? And what does 'proletarian' mean in this context?

Let's take each in turn. First, according to Gellius' Fronto, a writer can aspire to the title of 'classic' only if he is sufficiently ancient (*antiquior*). By definition, therefore, there cannot be modern classics, much less contemporary ones. So how is the adjective *classicus* being used here? How exactly is the metaphor applicable? We are fortunate in that elsewhere Gellius himself explains the precise meaning of the word. He tells us that 'not all those men who were enrolled in the five classes [of Servius Tullius] were called *classici*, but only the men of the first class, who were rated at a hundred and twenty-five asses or more. But those of the second class and of all the other classes, who were rated at a smaller sum than I have mentioned, were called "under class".'[58] Your 'class', in other words, would be determined by your status, or better, by your ranking in a census. A writer belonging to that 'earlier band' of the ancients has such extensive 'property' that he automatically falls within the highest class of citizens, just like a Roman aristocrat from a wealthy family of long standing.

If you are thinking that Gellius' 'classic' writer is someone who lives off a private income and behaves like a gentleman of leisure *yet* has to be 'assiduous' in his work, you are mistaken. For *assiduus* is another word linked to the census. It is Gellius once again who explains to us that '*assiduus* in the *Twelve Tables* is used of one who is rich and well-to-do'.[59] It's the same old story: the 'classic' writer is rich and carefree and has an easy life (*facile faciens*) – as one would expect of someone who belongs to the first of Servius' classes.

To conclude our investigation, let's look at what it means to be 'proletarian' – i.e. the sort of person, according to Gellius, whom there would be no point in asking whether he uses *harena* in the plural and *quadrigae* in the singular. Again, Gellius himself provides us with a definition, so we can be sure of what he means when he applies the term to writers. Once again we find ourselves in the midst of a discussion, this time about a passage in the *Twelve Tables* where the very word *proletarius* appears. Gellius and his friends first try to extract some information from a jurist, who unfortunately turns out to be rather ignorant. Next they turn to the poet Iulius Paulus, a man reputed to be the most learned of his entire generation – and he doesn't let them down. He proceeds to explain that *proletarii* were defined as the humblest and poorest of the Roman *plebs*, those who reported no more than one thousand five hundred *asses* at the census. Normally the Romans didn't bother to enrol proletarians in the army 'since property and money were regarded as a hostage and pledge of loyalty to the state, and since there was in them a kind of guarantee and assurance of patriotism'.[60] Only in times of great danger, when men of military age were scarce, were the poor enrolled among the emergency troops. In those circumstances they were enlisted under the title *proletarii*, which derived 'from their duty and function of producing offspring [*proles*], for although they could not greatly aid the state with what small property they had, yet they added to the population of their country by their power of begetting children'.[61]

113

So the non-classical writer would be one whose only contribution to the society of literature is through his offspring, or *proles*: his handicap is his lack of property, as a result of which he cannot offer the state any 'pledge of loyalty'. This is an important point. In Gellius' property metaphor classical writers are distinguished from non-classical precisely on the basis of their 'solvency'. A writer can aspire to the status of 'classical' only if he seems so trustworthy that anyone can turn to him to find out whether *harena* can be used in the plural and *quadrigae* in the singular. Look at all his property: he must be a classical writer. In a sense, he can always reimburse us if he makes a mistake. But how can one possibly trust a proletarian writer who can't even scrape together one thousand five hundred *asses*? The proletarian can offer no guarantee of any sort; he is not a person worthy of trust.

We can cite an even more learned text than that of Gellius: I refer to Paul the Deacon's epitome of the work *On the Meaning of Words*, originally composed by the grammarian Sextus Pompeius Festus. Above all, this citation will provide proof that the defining characteristic of anything *classicus* is precisely its capacity to offer surety, to guarantee its own assertions or actions. This ancient lexicon, at the entry *classici testes*, reads: 'those are defined as "classical" witnesses who are engaged to sign wills.'[62] Here again, in other words, the category 'classical' corresponds to the ability to guarantee – to the possession of authority and respectability. The classical writer is one who will not cheat you. He has a rich estate; you can be confident that you will always find him solvent. All things considered, Gellius' Fronto was nearer the truth than at first he seemed. One cannot deny that, across the span of our civilisation, the classics have often played an authoritative role. 'It was written by Plato', people say; 'I read it in Homer' – meaning that we are dealing with an outstanding witness; the information comes from a person of the first rank. By contrast, the proletarian writers – that is, the moderns – could never be cited in this way. They are simply producers of literary offspring, without property or status. You wouldn't think of asking them to witness your will.

... and moderns

Do not be alarmed. I am fully aware that I have already defined the classics as just something we happen to encounter, or 'bump into' along the way, and I will return to that in a moment. But I also promised to mention some more recent definitions of the classics. Here, then, is a brief selection. We can begin with Mark Twain's, by now a classic in itself: 'something that everybody wants to have read and nobody wants to read.' A definition so sharp it almost hurts, just like the truth. It makes sense, then, to follow it with the definition offered by Jorge Luis Borges in the course of his conversations with Osvaldo Ferrari: 'A classic ... is a book read with respect.'[63] Nice, but is it true? Many people read the classics with little or no respect; we've seen too many examples of them along our way. Next, at least two definitions from Eugenio Montale.[64] 'The classic is the character in whose absence part of the world would seem empty, uninhabited. A classic can take on a life of its own, from Homer to Shakespeare, even if the whole work or part of it never really existed.'[65] Here the classics divide the whole world up between them, and they can do this even when they don't really exist. In the second of Montale's definitions, he returns to the theme of 'occupying' something, but this time it's not a question of dividing up the world. 'In the history of great literature, the classics are the first to have arrived, those who occupy the best seats. Everybody else has to stand, and many of them will end up by going home.'[66] So the classics are compared to those who have occupied the front rows at the theatre, while all those who arrive later have to crane their necks to see or go straight back home. After the Greek trage-dians had written their plays, what was left for subsequent tragedians to do? Crane their necks; the classics had got there first. And the same holds for all other literary genres. This definition seems to me both profound and insightful, but the idea of exclusivity, or rather of exclusion, makes me uncom-fortable. Is it really true that the rest of us cannot find a seat if the classics are already there? If you reason in this way you'll end up endorsing the sentiments of Berchoux.

Then there are the definitions of the classic supplied by Italo Calvino, which may well be the most subtle and affec-tionate.[67] There are fourteen of them, but I have always found number eight the most appealing: 'A classic is a work which is always stirring up a dust-storm of critical debate around itself, only to shake it off later on.' This is a felicitous definition in that it makes you reflect on the fact that the so-called 'dust', with which many claim the classics are covered to such an extent as to render them illegible, in fact comes from outside. We interpreters throw it over them by the handful. But the classic is like a big friendly dog – eventually it just gives a shake and goes off to play with the children.

When it comes to the Greek and Latin classics, I still see them essentially as something that has always been there and that we are bound to encounter along the way. This is one of their most peculiar characteristics, if not the fundamental one. Ancient as they are, the classics are a unique category of texts which were already in existence when all other books had yet to be written. For this reason the classics have been read by a vast number of people over the course of time – far more than could possibly be the case with recent books. So the classics represent what we know we have in common with the generations that precede us. When one reads a classical text for the first time, one often has the impression that one already knows it. This is the case with familiar expressions, which one uses habitually without ever knowing where they come from. But it can also happen with ideas or literary allusions or with authors. One always has a lot of friends in common with the classics, and one never ceases to be amazed by that realisation. For instance, some people hate Latin writers or know very little about them, but are very fond of F. Scott Fitzgerald because he is American and modern. Later they find out that *The Great Gatsby*, as its author explicitly tells us, was originally going to be called *Trimalchio in West Egg*, or simply *Trimalchio*.[68] This inevitably casts a different light on how Fitzgerald construed the world, and especially the dinner parties, of the great Gatsby. And don't forget that Pasolini conceived his *Petrolio* as 'a modern Satyricon'.[69] I personally wouldn't rule out the possibility that 'Petrolio' was chosen as a pun to remind us of Petronio/Petronius.

A classic in one's lifetime?

Let's bid farewell to definitions of the classics and pick up the thread of a previous conversation. I was saying that the search for surprise and for mysteries to unveil now seems to dominate many aspects of our culture. The unexpected turn of events, the denouement, the sudden confession – the important thing is that the text throws off its mask in the end. Or, better still, that the person who wrote it does – the *author*.

Eugenio Montale is a much loved Italian poet of long standing. The poet and novelist Antonio Tabucchi[70] was inspired by Montale in choosing the title (and not only the title) of one of his collections of short stories; a poet friend of mine swears that he began to write poetry immediately after Montale's *Satura* was published. Many consider my friend a

117

good writer; it is apparent that he has learned well. Nor could it be otherwise, for someone who can write a line such as *il conto del telefono si e ridotto a ben poco* ('the phone bill has come down to almost nothing') to refer to the death of his wife Mosca has something to teach us all, and for generations to come.[71] Could Montale be called a classic? That might be going too far.

In any case, while Montale was alive he never achieved that status; his last columns in *Corriere della Sera* betrayed nothing of the smug posturing that usually characterises the 'living classic'. On the contrary. Anyway, it is always safer not to aspire to classic status while you're still alive. The case of the poet Cinna (first century BC) is exemplary: his poem, *Zmyrna*, was declared a classic as soon as it was published. Catullus praised it as incomparable;[72] it could hardly have been otherwise given that it took nine long years to complete (nine is also the number of the Muses).[73] Catullus was sure that *Zmyrna* would be read in the farthest reaches of the globe and that the centuries would become *cana*, that is, they would turn grey, before people ever ceased to read it. Naturally scholiasts and exegetes were involved, and scholars of every sort; the grammarian Crassicius made a name for himself in the field. And today? No one remembers Crassicius; no one remembers *Zmyrna*. We cannot even read it, for it has not been preserved and handed down to us. As a rule, it's better not to be declared a classic while you're still alive.

The age of indiscretion

Classic or no, Montale remains a great poet. Yet in recent years his fame seems to have been declining. When you hear his name mentioned these days it is only in the context of the revelation that, if I remember correctly, he commissioned others to write pieces which he then took credit for himself. After this, his fame quotient suddenly shot back up. Then, silence again. This is not an isolated occurrence. We are very interested in the authors of literary texts at the moment of revelation, and far less interested in our everyday relationship with their works. Their presence makes itself felt with the appearance of letters, memoirs, postcards, and so on. There is a great appetite nowadays for indiscretions and trivialities. To have written *il conto del telefono si e ridotto a ben poco* is important, of course, but how can it compare to the moment when someone finally declares that he has discovered the exact amount, to the penny, of that blessed phone bill? Yet Montale had foreseen it all. Back in 1972 he was already writing:

They are preparing the iconography
of the greatest writers and soon
also of the least great ...

we will touch their clothing, their bathrobes, their enemas
if used and when and how many, the hotel menus,
the signed IOUs, the lotions
or potions or decoctions, the length
of their affairs, spiritual or fleshly
or merely epistolary, we will read
clinical charts, test results, and learn whether they fell asleep
reading Baffo[74] or the Bible.
    In this way history
passes over wisdom for haemorrhoids ...[75]

The point is that wisdom rarely turns out to be surprising. It cannot be unmasked after a long pursuit. Wisdom is not a 'person' and our civilisation, as we have learned, has to 'personify' as much information as possible in order to move around inside the vast archive.

The revelatory biography has become a popular literary

genre. The mechanism is the same as ever – the thriller, the unexpected turn of events – except that this time the killer you want to unmask is no longer the 'meaning' of the text but the author himself. I have already given plenty of examples of these sorts of indiscretions, or revelations. Nowadays there are books and newspapers full of this sort of thing. I shall limit myself to the observation that, once we have moved from texts to authors, the final surprise or unmasking of the villain no longer conforms to the style of a simple thriller but is its very archetype, or 'proto'-thriller. Now the protagonists are no longer fictional characters: they have become identified with the authors who created them. Simply by living out their lives, authors have created the most thrilling 'proto-novel' – all the more intriguing because it takes shape before our very eyes: every day there's a fresh twist, a new and baffling detail.

In this literary proto-novel, in which the author, rather than the characters, plays the leading role, our culture takes its love of personification to extremes. You can put Montale's *Satura* back on the shelf and bring the 'person' of the poet directly to life on the screen, preferably accompanied by several of his contemporaries. We can't be bothered to read novels or poetry: the lines of orderly type tire our eyes. We want to talk to the men and women themselves. Television has introduced a whole new desire for speech in the rooms of the vast archive. The small screen is an inexhaustible source of faces, expressions, commentators chatting on sofas, journalists speaking to camera, people being interviewed at the scene of an incident. We have become accustomed to what one might call 'reading through dialogue'. Our culture, or perhaps I should say our acculturation, is ever more mediated by the 'speaking' presence of those who transmit it to us. That is why, consciously or not, we have recently started to reduce our vast archive to the spoken word, awakening within it as many faces and characters as we possibly can.

In the literary proto-novel, authors and fictional characters may even find themselves working side by side, actors in a single intricate plot. When we learn that the rape of Adela Quested by Dr Aziz actually took place in the original manuscript of *A Passage to India*, but was suppressed in the final draft of the novel, the plot of the proto-novel is so striking that we forget to ask: But to whom does this indiscretion refer? To Forster or to his characters? It makes no difference – it's the same thing. There's only one plot; the soap opera has its own momentum. The same thing has happened to historical figures who have been presumed to be the models for literary heroes. I'm willing to admit that Don Juan de Tarsiss y Peralta, the historical individual by whom Tirso de Molina may well have been inspired to write his *Burladór*, was homosexual. But what does that have to do with Tirso's Don Juan/Don Giovanni, or Molière's, or Da Ponte's? It has nothing to do with them, yet the characters of the proto-novel will feel its effects just the same. After such a revelation, such an indiscretion, nothing can ever be the same. The next production of Mozart's *Don Giovanni* will almost certainly have to take it into account.

One cannot deny that this continual blurring of the boundaries between the story in the text and the biography of the author, between literary heroes, writers, and historical figures, is strongly suggestive of television. On TV, fiction and live reportage blur into one. We have become accustomed to seeing everything mixed up together – the 'truth' of the news report and the fiction of whatever made-for-TV film follows the news; the real and the imaginary. They often behave in very similar ways. Recently there was a rumour that some TV reporters had been accused of paying militiamen from the former Yugoslavia to ambush someone live on camera, in order to make their report seem more realistic. Of course we all hope there was no truth to this rumour, but even without recourse to such deliberate falsification it still remains unclear, for example, to what extent most people are aware of the distinction between the actual war in southeast Asia and the events shown in the various *Rambo* films.

7

The Classics in an Age of Indiscretion

Real marksmen fire directly at the author: this is the 'royal shot' in the world of indiscretion. When finally unmasked, authors always turn out to be so much more exciting than their characters. Of course, unmasking Tiresias or acquitting Oedipus is in itself great marksmanship, as I have emphasised. But such feats are as nothing compared to the possibility of unmasking Sophocles himself. The attempt, however, will be fraught with difficulties.

There are few things that can be revealed about Sophocles, and they are essentially rather bland – at least to palates like ours, accustomed to spicier indiscretions. The biography of Sophocles written in ancient times and transmitted to us along with the text of his tragedies is very sparing with juicy details,[1] unless you are turned on by knowing that, after the victory at Salamis, the young Sophocles led a chorus of young boys, naked and accompanied only by the lyre; or that he died of choking on an unripe grape. We learn a few slightly more indiscreet details from Athenaeus, but nothing that would make it to the cover of a weekly news magazine. Athenaeus simply says that Sophocles loved young boys, while Euripides loved women.[2] After this he recounts a couple of anecdotes which begin with Sophocles' interest in a handsome young man but focus primarily on his presence of mind and refined literary judgement. No real indiscretion. And the same sort of thing could be said of Vergil too, though

123

to a lesser degree, for in his case, in fact, we do have a few indiscretions.

For instance, Suetonius, a relentless gossip[3] who would have been completely at home in our era, in his biography of Vergil related that the poet was particularly attracted to young boys, and that his favourites were called Cebes and Alexander.[4] It is Alexander who is celebrated in the second eclogue under the name Alexis. Vergil's affair with Plotia Hieria was widely rumoured; according to Vergil's biographer, Plotia herself said that her husband Varius Rufus urged Vergil to take her as his mistress, but Vergil refused.[5] We are thus discreetly informed about the sex life of the author, and this serves to sprinkle the *Eclogues* with a judicious quantity of rocket. Vergil also seems to have suffered from 'very slow speech' (*sermo tardissimus*), which meant that he was no good at public speaking and explains why he argued only a single case in court.[6] It is said that Philistus, one of Vergil's critics, nicknamed him *elinguis*, 'tongueless', because he never spoke in public. Until, one day, Vergil explained to Philistus that, if he needed to make a point in public, he could use the 'trumpet' (*tuba*) of Augustus and Maecenas whenever he liked.[7] Vergil gave Philistus a clever answer, yet there are probably those who will be delighted to hear that Vergil, the great poet of the *Aeneid*, couldn't speak in public. It's a revelation all right, a twist (albeit a minor one – it's not as if one had discovered that Pavarotti was a deaf mute as a child).

However, these ancient revelations are not always reliable. For instance, how are we to reconcile *that* anecdote with another contemporary report that Vergil had a voice of the sweetest timbre? Perhaps his voice was somewhat weak: in desperate situations, as when Vergil was reading the *Aeneid* to Augustus and his voice began to fail, the faithful Maecenas took his place. Nonetheless, his voice was the envy of many. The poet Iulius Montanus said, 'I would happily have stolen some of Vergil's lines, if only I could have stolen his voice too.'[8] This was because Vergil's poetry sounded right only when it came from his own lips; spoken by others it sounded flat and lifeless. But in that case why did Philistus call Vergil 'tongueless'? Something doesn't quite add up.

When one is in search of indiscretions, or better still, of gossip, it's a good idea to consult the detractors. Whether they attack their subject from envy, or because they were abused as children, or for whatever reason, they are always an inexhaustible source of revelations. They will remember the tiniest grain of truth in the slightest peccadillo. Otherwise they will make it up, and that is sometimes even better. Naturally Vergil had a host of detractors: they comprised a distinct group known as the *obtrectatores Vergilii* and were regularly denounced by various pro-Vergilian grammarians. Grammarians have always been a rather conservative lot. So let's look at another of Vergil's detractors. After the publication of the *Eclogues*, Numitorius responded to Vergil with his own *Anti-Eclogues*. Given the title, one immediately anticipates a selection of spicy details about Alexis or Corydon, but that does not prove to be the case.[9] I'll let you be the judge. In an attempt to parody the famous first line of the first eclogue (*Tityre tu patulae recubans sub tegmine fagi*; 'You, Tityrus, lying under the spreading shade of a beech tree'), Numitorius could only come up with this:

> *Tityre, si toga calda tibi est, quo 'tegmine fagi'?*
> 'Tityrus, if you have a warm toga, what's the "beech blanket" for?'

It's not easy to translate the line into English. Most likely, Numitorius thought that the word *tegmen* should be used only to describe something that covers the body (a cloak, dress, blanket, etc.). So he makes fun of Vergil for using *tegmen* to indicate the shade supplied by the canopy of a beech tree. Nit-picking grammarians! Even Donatus, who was also a grammarian, thought Numitorius' bucolic parody *insulsissima* (extremely stupid). And he's right: the business of a *toga calda* is extremely stupid, especially since, as is well-known, Tityrus almost certainly represents Vergil. A true *obtrectator* of the poet would have got straight to the point – he could have put it this way, for example:

> *Tityre tu patuli recubans sub tegmine phalli*
> 'You, Tityrus, lying under the spreading shade of an erect phallus'

and the door would have been open for all sorts of indiscreet suggestions about Vergil's libido as he lay in the shade of a huge Mantuan phallus. Instead Numitorius went off and created a 'warm toga'.

Fortunately things improve a little when the *obtrectatores Vergilii* move from attempts at parody to accusations of plagiarism, describing the poet's 'thefts' from the works of others. It seems that a certain Perellius Faustus specialised in the field of Vergilian plagiarism. Despite the loss of so many works of ancient poetry, a discreet list of Vergil's thefts (set out so that Vergil's passage is followed by that of his predecessor) can still be read in the section of Macrobius' *Saturnalia* dedicated to the appearance of ancient Roman writers in Vergil's poetry.[10] The only problem is that Rufius Albinus, the learned character in the dialogue to whom Macrobius entrusts the responsibility of dealing with this material, had no intention of classifying Vergil's various borrowings as plagiarism. Quite the contrary: according to Albinus they were 'flowers which he has plucked from them all – the decorative passages which he has taken from various sources to give beauty to his work'. In treating this delicate aspect of Vergil's poetry, Albinus was well aware that he could easily have 'offered ignorant or spiteful persons a starting point for their critique of Vergil', so he played it safe. Not only, he said, did all the Greek and Latin poets do exactly the same thing of which Vergil is accused, but these authors' impulse to draw on the work of others stemmed from a spirit of honest emulation, not from any desire to steal. Albinus adds: 'in fact they should be grateful to Vergil for doing this, since by transferring their work into his own he has ensured that these ancient writers will never be forgotten'. And it cannot be denied that Vergil will always be the best. 'Vergil chose with such good taste, and such was the manner of his imitation, that when, in our reading of him, we come across another's words, we either believe they are Vergil's own or else we marvel at how much better they sound than they did in the works from which they are taken.'

On the whole, Albinus was a bit of a hypocrite. Vergil copied from others yet, according to Albinus, he'd done those poor fellows a favour because he thereby ensured that works would be remembered which would never have survived on their own merits. But it is not quite true to say that he did his models a favour: he helped them to survive, true, but only so that people could say that the plagiarised was undoubtedly inferior to the plagiariser. Some favour – you survive only to be rated forever inferior to someone who, in the final analysis, copied your work. It would probably be better to have been lost forever. Let us hope that what we read next about Vergil in the *Vitae* isn't true.[11] One day Vergil was seen with a copy of Ennius' poetry in his hands. When someone asked him what he was doing, he is supposed to have replied: 'I am collecting gold from Ennius' shit.'

So from time to time the greatest Latin poet copied his fellow writers. That's rather like Horace saying that, now and then, even Homer nods. Even in Vergil's own time, strong language was used to describe his debts to the tradition: theft (*furta*),[12] wrongful use (*usurpatio*), even dishonesty (*fraus*).[13] Then commentators like Albinus come along and transform everything into a favour done to his predecessors. The classics, the truly great classics, often enjoy this privilege. They devour their own parents, and those parents are expected to be grateful to them. If anyone dares to reproach them, even in a respectful way, they reply: Are you implying that I stole a line from Homer? Try it yourself. Stealing a line from Homer is like stealing Hercules' club.[14] And off they go.

One cannot deny that, despite much reticence and a thousand difficulties, we have managed to put together some indiscretions about Vergil. As you can see, the art of indiscretion was also practised by the ancients – though not with the force imposed by the development of the mass media. But despite our apparent success, we are still a long way from achieving our goal. Let us take the case of Vergil's love for young boys. The indiscretion before us seems enticing, but it is soon revealed as wholly insipid. Who in fact *are* Cebes and Alexander? Even if you could verify that the beloved face of Alexander is concealed beneath the mask to Alexis in the second eclogue, that revelation goes nowhere. For Alexander is still a complete unknown. A proper indiscretion requires some kind of notoriety. No one is interested in revelations about strangers or unimportant people. For us to be genuinely interested in this Alexander, we need to be told, for example, that he was the son of Cornelius Gallus.[15] If Plotia Hieria's affair with Vergil is to be exciting, a letter or diary needs to be found which identifies her as the wife of Augustus.

But none of this will happen. In the world of the classics there are no ageing lovers to interview, no archives for heirs to auction off or drawers for them to rifle through. Even if there was once something, it has gone. Anyway, I seriously doubt that, even in Vergil's own time, there was much damaging material in circulation about him. We do have some material of this sort about the classics – no argument – and sooner or later someone will collect it in a stimulating little volume. But for this to be transformed into a culture of indiscretion, or a novel, or a soap opera, as we've become accustomed to nowadays, there is a vital ingredient which will always be missing – namely the possibility of adding to the legacy of indiscretions that we already possess. We do this by contradicting some, by embellishing others, by continually adding new characters and unexpected twists to the plot. In this respect classical texts are absolutely unchanging. Of course there are new interpretations, incisive critiques, and more or less rigorous analyses. But these sorts of indiscretions, even those championed by well-respected scholars, never turn out entirely satisfying. This is because an indiscretion, to be really efficacious, needs documentation, whether authentic or forged, not conjecture.

We will never succeed in writing a metanovel about the classics. That's another basic difference between classical authors and all the others. Classical authors are defined as such precisely on the basis that it's very difficult, if not impossible, to come up with continual revelations about them. Serene in their 'spaces between the worlds' (*intermundia*), like the Epicurean gods, they enjoy peaceful privacy: no director will ever come and knock on their door to ask them to play a role in a soap opera inspired by indiscreet literature. We don't even know when most of them were born. The biography of Homer is so elusive that the poet of that name probably never existed. The classics stubbornly refuse to enter the age of indiscretion. And that is no coincidence. It is not due to the fact that time has destroyed exciting revelations. It is actually more reasonable to assume that classical authors knew perfectly well how things would turn out, and that they deliberately made themselves safe from any denigration of their character. And this will be the subject of the Epilogue.

Epilogue

The Indiscretions of the Written Word

A sword to a child

Clement of Alexandria, a Christian writer of the second century, began his *Miscellanies* by asking himself: 'Should everyone be denied the right to leave behind writings (*syngrammata*), or should that right be allowed to a few? If the former, what is the point of writing? If the latter, should the worthy or the unworthy be allowed to do so? It would plainly be ridiculous to reject the writing of authors who are worthwhile and reject the writing of those who are not.'[1] Clement had a rather elitist attitude to writing, and he had a similar approach to reading. Later, he claims that 'if true knowledge cannot be revealed to everyone, then to put the writings before the man in the street is, in the proverbial phrase, "to give a lyre to a donkey" '.[2] When you are about to read a work written by someone else you should be aware that, by doing so, you are very much like someone who is about to take communion: 'normally it is left to each member of the congregation to decide whether to take part.'[3] In other words, the act of reading is a serious responsibility, just like the act of writing, which Clement restricts to *spoudaioi*, respectable people.

The point is that culture, that immense legacy left to whoever wishes to take advantage of it, is transmitted in two ways: the written and the spoken. Alluding to the Gospel, Clement expresses himself in a more figurative way: 'The harvest is plentiful, the labourers few ... the cultivation is of two kinds: one uses writing, the other doesn't.'[4] Clement finds culture/cultivation that is not written down, by which I mean oral transmission of knowledge, much safer than that which *is* written down. He believes this because 'the person who addresses people who are present uses time as a test and judgment to come to a verdict. He distinguishes the ones who are capable of hearing him from the rest. He keeps an eye on their words and ways, their character and life, their impulses and attitudes, their looks, their voice ....'[5] What happens, on the other hand, to the person who addresses himself not to listeners but to readers? 'The person who uses the written word for communication hallows it before God by proclaiming in writing that he is not writing for profit or vainglory; that he is not overpowered by emotion, a slave to fear, or exulting in pleasure; that his sole delight is in the salvation of those who encounter his writings. In that salvation he does not claim any present share. He receives in hope the change that will be granted ....'[6] Directly addressing an audience, then, is much better than sending written words to one who is not present. But Clement realises that the spoken word has its limitations too. He is aware that 'many things have passed away from us into oblivion in a long lapse of time through not being written down'.[7] For that reason, and not without a certain reluctance, he decided to write down those things that ran the risk of growing ever fainter and eventually disappearing altogether because they were preserved only in his memory. Still, he did so with the following proviso: 'out of fear of writing what I have refrained from speaking – not in a grudging spirit (that would be wrong) but in the fear that my companions might misunderstand [my writings] and go astray and that I might be found "offering a sword to a child" (as those who write proverbs put it). Once a thing is written, there is no way of keeping it from the public, even if it remains unpublished by me, and in its scrolls it employs no voice other than its own forever. It can make no response to a questioner beyond what is written. It cannot help needing support either from the writer or some other person following in his footsteps.'[8]

This text is striking. To our eyes, a piece of writing is not as disturbing an object as it obviously was to Clement. His images are forceful. Writing seen as 'a sword to a child', for instance, suggests the idea that the letters of the alphabet are somehow sharp and cutting, and should be handled with care. Meanwhile, the sense of inevitability that pervades a phrase such as 'once a thing is written, there is no way of keeping it from the public, even if it remains unpublished by me' makes you wonder whether the letters of the alphabet are capable of cutting not only the hands of the person who unrolls the scroll but also those of the person who has been rash enough to write on it. At this point, however, I must add that the (not always terribly lucid) ideas that Clement develops concerning the deficiencies of writing merely take up the same position that a philosopher far greater than he had elaborated more than five centuries earlier – apart from the proverbs, that is.

I am referring, of course, to Plato. In the last paragraph that I quoted from Clement, he restates Plato's ideas almost verbatim. Plato dealt with writing in at least two passages of his *Letters* and in an even more famous passage in the *Phaedrus*. Let us begin with *Letter* VII, which Plato sent to the friends and relatives of Dio, in which he expresses his annoyance at reports that Dionysius II had tried to put down in writing the instructions that Plato had given him and then had the gall to pass the whole thing off as his own work. Plato felt obliged to explain in detail the 'true reasoning' which precludes any possibility of giving written form to his teaching. But contrary to what one might expect, what follows in the letter does not comprise a denunciation of plagiarism but a most appealing theory of learning.[9]

Knowledge, Plato explains, is the result of five essential factors, whose interaction yields understanding. But how do you attain that understanding?

It is by means of the examination of each of these objects, comparing one with another ... proving them by kindly proofs and employing questions and answers that are void of envy – it is by such means, and hardly so, that there bursts out the light of intelligence and reason regarding each object in the mind of he who uses every effort of which mankind is capable. And this is the reason why every serious person in dealing with really serious objects avoids writing, lest thereby he may possibly cast them as a prey to the envy and stupidity of the public. In one word, then, our conclusion must be that whenever one sees a person's written compositions – whether they be the laws of a legislator or anything else in any other form – these are not his most serious works, even if the writer himself is serious: rather those works abide in the fairest region he possesses (namely, in the mind). If, however, these really are serious efforts, and put into writing, it is not 'the gods' but mortal men who 'then of a truth themselves have utterly ruined his senses'.[10]

Thus knowledge is a flash, a spark resulting from mutual friction between the five factors involved in oral discussion. But a flash cannot be written down. If one commits to writing the process which should lead, during the course of discussion, to the creation of this flash, one only exposes one's own 'serious things' to the envy and ignorance of others. At most, writing can function as a trace, as a memorandum.[11] But no respectable person would ever think of consigning true knowledge to the letters of the alphabet.

How different is our own conception of culture when compared to that of Plato. For us, serious things, or at least those considered to be serious, are the ones that are written down. For him it was exactly the opposite. The point is that for centuries we have become accustomed to believe that the flash of comprehension must appear at the moment we underscore a line of text we are reading. That is why, whether the flash appears as a solitary light inside us or in discussion with others, the first thing we feel we have to do is to transfer the entire experience onto a sheet of paper.

The reflections on writing that Plato developed in *Letter VII* are very close to those that appear at the end of the *Phaedrus*.[12] Here too, the philosopher closely analyses the risks and shortcomings inherent in using the letters of the alphabet, but the perspective he chooses has much greater relevance for us that the preceding one. Socrates has just finished telling Phaedrus the Egyptian myth of Thoth, the god who invented the letters of the alphabet. Thoth's invention was rejected by the wise king Thamus, who argues that writing would not prove capable to transmitting the truth of wisdom, only its appearance. Socrates then adds:

> writing ... has this strange quality, and is very like painting; for the creatures of painting stand like living beings, but if one asks them a question, they preserve a solemn silence. And so it is with written words; you might think they spoke as if they had intelligence, but if you question them, wishing to know about their sayings, they always say only one and the same thing.

Thus the written word is inaccurate and misleading; it simulates the appearance of real insight just as a painting of living things simulates the appearance of real life. A painted image and a written symbol are associated with the usual Platonic condemnation of whatever inadequately reproduces otherwise 'true' beings. But now we have reached the point of greatest interest: the risks to which written imita-

135

tion of spoken discourse subjects the living material repli-
cated in it.

> And every word, when once it is written [Socrates continues],
> is bandied about, alike among those who understand and
> those who have no interest in it, and it knows not to whom to
> speak or not to speak; when ill-treated or unjustly reviled it
> always needs its father to help it; for it has no power to protect
> or help itself .... Now tell me; is there not another kind of
> speech, or word, which shows itself to be the legitimate
> brother of this bastard one, both in the manner of its begetting
> and in its better and more powerful nature? ... The word which
> is written with intelligence in the mind of the learner, which is
> able to defend itself and knows to whom it should speak, and
> before whom to be silent?

The dangers to which writing exposes the life of the discourse
are thus the promiscuity of potential liaisons, insults, and the
inability to defend itself. Reproduced in its written image, the
'true' discourse not only loses its own capacity to reply to the
questions put to it (and thus the capacity to signify anything
beyond what is strictly contained in it), but, like a child
without a father, exposes its own vital substance to all the
dangers of neglect and abandonment. Plato understood
extremely well that our culture, once reduced to 'text', could
then be subjected to insults. The letters of the alphabet
certainly have an extraordinary power to conserve what has
been entrusted to them. Without them, for instance, we could
not read the *Phaedrus* or Homer or Vergil. The classics would
not exist, and we would not be here discussing them. Thanks
to the alphabet, the classics *do* exist, but that sublime result
has not been achieved without cost. Once written, books can
get into anybody's hands – and not only books: anything at
all, once it has been written down, is common property and
can pass into anyone's hands, even those of the indiscreet.

This shortcoming leads us directly to Plato's second letter, a text that develops the theme of writing and its dangers. Here Plato (or more likely an impostor who took the trouble to imitate him)[13] is worried about the possibility that the letter he has addressed to Dio will 'end up in the hands of uneducated people'.[14] He goes on to speak of the teachings he has imparted to Dio, and warns him to 'have care lest one day you should repent of what has now been divulged improperly. The greatest safeguard is to avoid writing and to learn by heart; for it is not possible that what is written down should not get divulged. For this reason, I myself have never yet written anything on these subjects .... Read this letter over repeatedly and then burn it.'

The author of this letter, whoever he was, certainly manifests a deep-seated fear of the letters of the alphabet. He fears them, and he rejects them as an aid to the diffusion of his teaching. Yet at the very same time he is using them to tell Dio that he has rejected writing: burn this letter! As I have already mentioned, the person who wrote this letter was almost certainly an impostor, but at least he is honest and explicit about the paradox that all denunciations of writing, when expressed in writing, inevitably represent. To escape from this awkward situation, the writer must do one of two things after he has finished his argument: either he must destroy what he has written about the harm he feels writing causes, or he must ask the addressee to destroy it – which is precisely what the author of the second letter of Plato did. Of course, the best thing would have been to criticise writing orally, demonstrating through action, pragmatically, just how deeply you detest the means of expression you are denouncing. But if you do that all the rest of us who are not taking part in the dialogue could never be informed of the harm that writing causes. A neat paradox: you denounce writing while simultaneously trying to assure the greatest possible circulation for your personal dislikes – which inevitably means doing so in writing.

The author of this letter says something that is of great interest from the very perspective that intrigues us, that of indiscretion. When he makes the peremptory statement: 'it is impossible to avoid debasing what is written down', this is the same phrase that caught Clement's attention. Classical authors, if I can put it this way, were afraid of any indiscretion. And they were clearly aware of the way in which an indiscretion comes about and of its principal cause – the channel which best fosters its diffusion: writing. Sooner or later, what is written down circulates, is read and comes to be known. The point is that writing authorises reading; in some ways it actually demands it. If you see a book, a newspaper, a piece of paper, you immediately feel authorised to pick it up and read it. We are accustomed to do this; the letters of the alphabet, or the process of progressively reducing our culture to 'text', were invented precisely as tools for communication. They are an open dialogue that persistently seeks an interlocutor. How can you ask writing to abstain from doing what it was designed to do – namely, offer itself to be read? Certainly there are writings and then there are writings. A letter such as the one sent to Dio is, at least in theory, for Dio alone. But as soon as something has been written down, it becomes extremely difficult to claim that it was written only for a certain person or only for us and no one else, while other things are written for general consumption. That is why Dio was asked to burn the letter. With the passage of time, some expressions of politeness or reserve, placed more or less explicitly at the beginning of texts, tend to be deleted. When you decide to write something down, no matter what it is, you must be aware that just as reading cannot exist without writing, no more can writing exist without reading.

It is different when two people speak to one another. From

this point of view, Clement describes the advantages of spoken discourse very well: when you converse, you can choose your interlocutor and look him straight in the eye. Spoken discourse is not addressed to someone you just happened to meet in passing; in order to listen or respond, you have to be authorised. It is considered impolite to move close so that you can listen in on a conversation – that makes everyone uncomfortable and produces embarrassing moments of silence. It is, in fact, considered extremely indiscreet. When one of Plautus' characters is worried that there is someone hiding nearby hoping to eavesdrop on a conversation without being seen, he uses a special and very significant verb to encapsulate his anxiety: *aucupo*. For example, *numquis est sermones nostrum qui aucupet*? ('Is there anyone around to "catch" our conversation?').[15] But 'catch' only partially renders the meaning of *aucupo*. The verb literally denotes a method of catching birds by creeping up on them armed with a stick covered in birdlime. Then you frighten them and, as they take flight, they become entangled in the stickiness of the birdlime. In other words, you catch conversations in flight by using a trick, just as with the birds. Moreover, the etymology of the verb *aucupo* leads us directly to *avem capere*, 'to catch a bird'. Other people's conversations are caught by trickery, just like those poor little birds who would have flown away immediately if only they had known what was being planned behind their backs.

Plautus' metaphor is very pertinent: it is well-known that words (when spoken) have wings. In order to catch them in flight you have to proceed with the cunning of a fowler or you will never be able to hear what is none of your business. Thanks to Clement, we already know that speaking your words affords you the time and opportunity to look your interlocutor in the eye, and it also allows you to be silent, if you consider that a more prudent course. Written words, on

the other hand, do not fly off. Once they are written down –
like it or not – there is no longer any way to look your interlocutor in the eye. Texts are opened and read. That's why
Plato – the real one and the impostor – was so worried about
giving written form to something anyone could read. From
that moment on, his argument would be available to those
who were worthy of it and to those who were not. Like a
wretched orphaned child, it would have no one to turn to for
help, would not know to whom it should address itself. There
it is, 'ill-treated and unjustly reviled'. When discourse has
been reduced to text it is available to increasing numbers of
readers, theoretically without limit. Anyone who wants to
'catch' it no longer has to sneak around behind those in
conversation, like Plautus' fowler, but is authorised to do so
in the open with the full consent of the community.

Once written down, words are not only in the public
domain, but, worse, they are almost begging to be 'caught'.
Oral culture is a very discreet culture; written culture is
unavoidably indiscreet. You might even say that in building
the most monumental work of our tradition – the vast archive
– we have inevitably given life to the 'vast indiscretion' as
well. The more that is written, the more material we pile up
for potentially indiscreet use. Today, the child does indeed
have a sword in his hands. We can only hope that he does not
cut himself – or anyone else, for that matter.

The prison-house of civilisation

To be perfectly honest, I find Clement's sword a rather over-
powering metaphor for the letters of the alphabet. And yet
the Greek tradition about writing has preserved even more
striking reflections for our consideration. Let me return one
last time to Homer. When Anteia, wife of Proetus, fell in love
with Bellerophon, it probably never crossed her mind that the

hero would refuse her. But he did, and she decided to take her revenge. She lied, as Phaedra had done, and told her husband that the young man had attempted to rape her. Filled with rage, Proetus wanted to punish Bellerophon, but was afraid to kill him himself:[16]

> But he sent him away to Lycia, and handed him murderous symbols
> which he inscribed in a folding tablet, enough to destroy life,
> and told him to show it to his wife's father, that he might perish.

In Lycia, Bellerophon was warmly welcomed by Proetus' father-in-law, the father of the wicked Anteia. But ten days later, when the king asked Bellerophon to show him the message from Proetus and read it, he immediately sent the hero to fight against the dreaded Chimaera. Bellerophon managed to kill the monster. After that he had to fight the Solymi, then the Amazons, and so on in a series of ever more dangerous trials. However, the most interesting aspect of this Homeric episode lies not in the epic narrative of a hero's accomplishments but in Proetus' message. This is in fact the only place in the Homeric poems where writing is specifically mentioned, and you have to admit that the context in which it appears is not entirely reassuring.

The *sêmata* ('symbols') inscribed on the folding tablet are explicitly called *lygra* ('deadly', 'murderous'). Of course this might be only an isolated case. Nevertheless I find it striking that, in a poetic tradition born in an oral context, the only reference to writing is to the murderous symbols drawn by Proetus. It seems that writing does not bode well for the person who is 'written down'. For the person who is the object of the message, let alone its unwitting bearer, the symbols on the folding tablet are a sentence of death.

The Greek hero could have provided bitter confirmation of the conclusions reached many years later by the Nambikuara, a group of Brazilian Amerindians studied by Claude Lévi-Strauss, when writing was introduced for the first time into their community. They were convinced that 'writing and deception had arrived in their midst together'.[17]

Bellerophon is a prisoner of writing. The *sêmata* of Proetus, once drawn and enclosed *en pinaki ptykôi*, turn out to be his death sentence, and the folding tablet springs on him like a trap. This recalls the 'spring' of the mythical magic mirror, which also folds up, enclosing the image of the person reflected and imprisoning it with no possibility of escape.[18] The victim is then no longer his own master, but utterly at the mercy of the one who possesses the mirror. In the myth of Proetus and Bellerophon, the written letters are represented as something that 'binds' the victim, putting him in the hands of the reader. Proetus has used the tablet on which Bellerophon's name is inscribed to take possession of the hero's very life. It is as though he has imprisoned his image.

The things that are written about us are not neutral representations. In a way they are equivalent to unprotected parts of our body or to images so closely connected to our person that they are directly identified with it. The Pythagoreans, those scrupulous custodians of ancient tradition, recommended that you should not leave hair trimmings or nail clippings lying about lest someone use them to exercise influence over your entire person. In the same way, they felt that you should erase your body's impression from your bed as soon as you got up in the morning.[19] That impression, like a shadow, is somehow 'part' of us. A silhouette can recall in its entirety the person who projects or imprints it. In other words, the Pythagoreans knew that our symbols, whatever form they take – traces of our physical reality, reflected images, or impressions – have the secret power to place us at the mercy of anyone who comes into their possession. So it is with writing, the most powerful tool we possess for the representation and conservation of our culture, but, by the same token, a folding mirror that delivers a final verdict. In the course of time, we have multiplied our impressions and our shadows, entrusting them to the letters of the alphabet. And now, in the vast archive that we have slowly built up over the course of centuries, the body of our culture is enclosed.

Notes

1. The Age of Futility

1. Seneca *Epistulae ad Lucilium* 88.39. [tr. R.L.]

2. Seneca *De brevitate vitae* 13.2-6. [tr. R.L.]

3. Jorge Luis Borges, *El Aleph* (Buenos Aires: Losada, 1959), English translation by Norman Thomas de Giovanni, *The Aleph and Other Stories, 1933-1969, Together with Commentaries and an Autobiographical Essay* (New York: E.P. Dutton, 1970), 15-30.

2. The Tyranny of Time

1. Axel Olrik, 'Epic laws of folk narrative', in Alan Dundes, *The Study of Folklore* (Englewood Cliffs, N.J.: Prentice Hall, 1965), 129-41.

2. This is obviously a totally arbitrary point of departure which you can change later in keeping with your own specific preferences or special purposes.

3. *De natura hominis* 38 in Migne, *Patrologia Graeca* 40: 760-1; and in Hans Friedrich August Von Arnim, ed., *Stoicorum Veterum Fragmenta* (Leipzig: Teubner, 1903-24), 2: 190 (625).

4. The famous accusers of Socrates.

5. *Adversus Graecos* 5 in Von Arnim, *SVF* 1: 32 (109). Greek text and English translation in Tatian, 'Oratio ad Graecos' and Fragments, ed. and tr. Molly Whittaker, *Oxford Early Christian Texts* (Oxford: Clarendon, 1982), 6-7.

6. Hesiod *Theogony* 53-63.

7. Caesar *Gallic War* 6.14.

8. Augustine *Confessions* 10.8 (12). [tr. R.L.]

9. Depending on the sex of the celebrand – *genius* for a male; *iuno* for a female.

10. *Rhetorica ad Herennium* 4.53.66: 'Personification (*conformatio*) consists ... in making a mute thing or one lacking form articulate, or attributing to it a definite form and a language or a certain behaviour appropriate to its character.' English translation by Harry Caplan for the Loeb Classical Library (London: Heinemann and Cambridge Ma.: Harvard University Press, 1964), 399.

144

11. Cicero *In Catilinam* 1.11.27. English translation by Louis E. Lord for the Loeb Classical Library (London: Heinemann and Cambridge Ma.: Harvard University Press, 1937), 41.

12. Isidore of Seville *Etymologies* 2.13.1-2.

3. The Urge for Instant Gratification

1. Epicurus *Epistula ad Menoeceum* 131b.

2. Carlo Battisti and Giovanni Alessio, *Dizionario etimologico italiano* (Florence: V. Barbera, 1957), *s.v.* The dictionary of Giacomo Devoto doesn't even have an entry for *sfizio*.

3. Norma Sparancari & Nzuddi, *Viaggio gastronomico di un linguista a Catania* (Rome: Signorelli, 1972), 42. I owe this reference to my friend Luciano Modica.

4. Jacques Gélis, *L'arbre et le fruit* (Paris: Fayard, 1984). English translation by Rosemary Harris, *History of Childbirth: Fertility, Pregnancy and Birth in Early Modern Europe* (Boston: Northeastern University Press, 1991), 57.

5. James G. Frazer, *Totemism and Exogamy*, 4 vols (London: Macmillan, 1910), 2: 106ff. Claude Lévi-Strauss, *La pensée sauvage* (Paris: Plon, 1962), English translation, *The Savage Mind*, Nature of Human Society Series (Chicago: University of Chicago Press and London: Weidenfeld and Nicolson, 1966), esp. 76-8.

6. Aristophanes *Peace*, scholion on line 497, *Scholia in Aristophanem*, part 2, fascicle 2, *Scholia vetera et recentiora in Aristophanis Pacem*, ed. D. Holwerda (Groningen: Bouma's Boekhuis, 1982), 81.

7. An interesting discussion of this can be found in Antonio Rosario Mennona, *Un dialetto della Lucania: Studi su Muro Lucano* (Galatina: Congedo, 1977), 2: 183; and Rainer Bigalke, *Dizionario dialettale della Basilicata* (Heidelberg: Winter, 1980), 754.

8. '... *cum maledictis ac probris*', Pliny the Elder *Natural History* 19.36.120.

9. Ibid. 20.39.101.

10. Augustine *City of God* 7.16, 21.

11. Liber was the Italic god of fertility and particularly of wine, and was commonly identified with the Greek Dionysus. Ceres was the Italic goddess of corn and was commonly identified with the Greek Demeter.

12. See, for instance, *Moretum* 84, *Appendix Vergiliana* ed. W.V. Clausen, F.R.D. Goodyear, E.J. Kenney and J.A. Richmonds (Oxford: Clarendon, 1966), 162; Columella *Res rustica* 10.105ff.; Martial *Epigrams* 3.75; and Juvenal *Satires* 9.134.

13. Ovid *Remedia amoris* 799.

14. Pliny the Elder *Natural History* 10.83.182. [tr. R.L.]

15. Ibid. 19.44.154-5.

16. *Geoponica* 12.13.2.

17. Marcel Detienne, *Les jardins d'Adonis* (Paris: Gallimard, 1972), English translation by Janet Lloyd, *The Gardens of Adonis: Spices in Greek Mythology* (Atlantic Highlands, N.J.: Humanities Press, 1971), 67-71.

18. *Moretum* 76, *Appendix Vergiliana* ed. Clausen et al., 161; Martial *Epigrams* 11.53.

19. Pliny the Elder, *Natural History* 19.38.128.

20. Columella *Res Rustica* 10.108.

21. In English, of course, the word 'rocket' also designates the probing space ship or missile, associated with the phallus and aggressive masculinity, as well as being a symbol of the modern age. [R.L.]

22. Lucian of Samosata (*c.* 117 – *c.* 180) wrote *A True Story* as a parody of fantastic tales of adventure. The *Metamorphoses* of Apuleius (born *c.* AD 123) narrate the amazing exploits of a young man called Lucius after he had been transformed into an ass. Both works cleverly combine humour and eroticism.

23. Plutarch *Vita Crassi* 32.3-4.

24. Gerhard Fink, *Ditelo in latino*, Italian trans. (Milan: Longanesi: 1992).

25. Giuseppe Gioachino Belli (1791-1863) was an Italian poet who wrote in the Roman dialect. Pier Paolo Pasolini (1912-75) wrote novels and poetry and directed films.

26. A series of short cheap classic works of literature, much like Penguin 60s, which cost 'mille lire' – a thousand lire or about 60p. [R.L.]

27. Danilus Poggiolinus is the Latinised form of Danilo Poggiolini, an Italian professor recently indicted in a scandal involving kickbacks on the sale of prescription drugs.

28. As a prominent leader of the Christian Democratic Party and several times Prime Minister beginning in 1972, Giulio Andreotti (1919-) is one of Italy's best-known politicians. Always a controversial figure, Andreotti went on trial in 1996 on charges of Mafia activities and conspiracy to murder a political journalist.

29. I take the examples that follow from a most unusual book by Hans Weis, *Bella Bulla: Lateinische Sprachspielerien* (Bonn: Dümmlers, 1985).

30. This letter and others that diffuse the legend of the presumed madness of the philosopher (10-17) are found in the *Oeuvres complètes* of Hippocrates edited by Emile Littré, vol. 9, *Lettres, decrets et harangues* (Paris: Ballière, 1861). They were forged in antiquity: see Hippocrates, *Sul riso e la follia*, ed. Yves Hersant (Palermo: Sellerio, 1991).

31. Ferdinand de Saussure (1857-1913) was a Swiss linguist whose ideas on the structure of language helped to establish the science of linguistics.

32. 'The Emperor and the Drummer' from *Ideas, The Book Le Grand,*

1826, in Heinrich Heine, *Works of Prose*, ed. Hermann Kesten (New York: L.B. Fischer, 1943), 228.

4. Belated Invocation

1. In the Italian original this invocation is addressed to Superio, a word which can be pronounced in two ways with two meanings. In the first case the word is pronounced with the stress on the second syllable, superio, and means 'superior one' or 'higher one' from the Latin *superior* (higher), i.e. 'Our Lord'. In the second case it is pronounced in two parts, super-io, and means 'super-ego'. It is up to the reader to choose which is meant here. [R.L.]

5. Time and the Canon

1. Fernando Sor (1778-1839) was a virtuoso Spanish guitarist, while Luis Milan (*c.* 1500 – after 1561) was a Spanish courtier and composer.

2. Heitor Villa-Lobos (1887-1959) was a Brazilian composer who was strongly influenced by the folk traditions of his native country.

3. Aulus Persius Flaccus (AD 34-62) was a Roman satirist of Stoic convictions. Publius Annius Florus (*fl. c.* AD 117-38) left only a short history of Rome, and it is virtually impossible to pass judgement on the quality of his writing.

4. Propertius *Elegiae* 3.3.1-4. English translation by G.P. Goold for the Loeb Classical Library (London: Heinemann and Cambridge, Ma.: Harvard University Press, 1990), 259. Mount Helicon, the highest peak in east central Greece (Boeotia), was supposed to be the abode of Apollo and the Muses.

5. Ezra Pound, 'Homage to Sextus Propertius' 2.76, *in Personae*: *The Shorter Poems of Ezra Pound*, ed. Lea Baechler and A. Walton Litz (New York: New Directions, 1990). The text was first published in 1913.

6. W.G. Hale, 'Pegasus Impounded', *Poetry* (1919), xiv, 52-5, reprinted in *Ezra Pound*: *The Critical Heritage*, ed. Eric Homberger (London: Routledge and Kegan Paul, 1972), 155-7.

7. Propertius *Elegiae* 3.3.48.

8. Pound, 'Homage' 1.58 and 2.130.

9. Propertius *Elegiae* 3.2.13.

10. Pound 'Homage' 1.56-8.

11. Alcinous was the mythical king of the Phaeacians and father of Nausicaa. He gave Odysseus hospitality and then sent him on to Ithaca on one of his magical ships.

12. Memorandum to A.R. Orage, editor of the *New Age* of London, who published between June and August 1919 the sections of the poem that did

not appear in *Poetry* (*The Letters of Ezra Pound 1907-1941*, ed. D.D. Paige (London: Faber & Faber, 1951), 212-13.

13. Ezra Pound, *Cathay*: *For the Most Part from the Chinese of Rihaku, from the Notes of the late Ernest Fenollosa, and the Decipherings of Professors Mori and Ariga* (1915).

14. Ford Madox Ford, 'From China to Peru', *The Outlook*, 19 June 1915. Repr. in *The Ford Madox Ford Reader*, ed. Sondra J. Stang (Manchester: Carcanet, 1986), 182-6, esp. 182. The critic, however, hastened to add: '... if these are original verses, then Mr Pound is the greatest poet of this day.' A judgement shared, I believe, by all readers of *Cathay*.

15. 'The Beautiful Toilet', in Pound, *Personae*, 132.

16. Propertius *Elegiae* 3.1.30 (tr. Goold).

17. Pound, 'Homage', 1.31.

18. Propertius *Elegiae* 2.2.11 (tr. Goold).

19. Pound, 'Homage', 1.31. The Taenarian promontory was the southernmost of the Peloponnese.

20. Propertius *Elegiae* 2.2.11 (tr. Goold): 'but if my journey were to result in certain funeral.'

21. Memorandum to A.R. Orage in *Letters 1907-1941*, ed. Paige, 211.

22. Ibid., 23ff. Pound's response to Adrian Collins is also cited in J.P. Sullivan, *Ezra Pound and Sextus Propertius*: *A Study in Creative Translation* (Austin: University of Texas Press, 1964), 9.

23. Ibid., 15.

24. Orosius *Historia* 1.18.1 (*Historiarum adversus paganos libri VII*, Vienna, 1882, repr. Hildesheim: Georg Olms, 1967). English translation by Ray J. Deferrari, *The Seven Books of History Against the Pagans*, The Fathers of the Church 50 (Washington, D.C.: Catholic University of America Press, 1964), 38.

25. Ibid., 93.

26. Alain René le Sage, *Histoire de Gil Blas de Santillane*, Book 2, ch. 9, English translation by T. Smollet, *The Adventures of Gil Blas of Santillane* (Philadelphia: J.B. Lippincott, 1867), 93-4. Diego was a barber who played the guitar.

27. The observation is by Alessandro Fo in his introduction to Rutilio Namaziano, *Il ritorno* (Turin: Einaudi, 1993), viii (one of the most beautiful translations of a poetic Latin text that has been published in recent years).

28. To be accurate, this line should not be attributed to Berchoux. In fact it seems that Jean Marie Bernard Clément, fully twenty-five years before Berchoux, had already cursed the classics in words very like those of Berchoux – except that, in place of the 'me' used by Berchoux (the egoist), Clément used a more discreet 'us'.

Notes

6. The Search for the Classics

1. Frederick M. Ahl, *Sophocles' Oedipus: Evidence and Self-Conviction* (Ithaca and London: Cornell University Press, 1991).

2. A.D. Fitton Brown, 'The Unreality of Ovid's Tomitan Exile', *Liverpool Classical Monthly* 10 (1985), 18-22.

3. Data referring to 1979 (in Fitton Brown, 'The Unreality', 18).

4. Dr Ernest Bonnejoy (du Vexin), *Le Végétarisme et le régime végétarien rationel: dogmatisme, histoire, pratique* (Paris: Baillière, 1891), 149ff: c'était blâmer ouvertement les usages nécrophagiques de la cour; aussi, la disgrâce du prince l'atteignit. Mais comme cela arrive souvent dans ce milieu, de tout temps voué à la fausseté et à tous les vices de nécrophagisme, ce ne fut pas, sans doute, la véritable raison qu'Auguste mit en avant; et, de nos jours encore, l'obscurité règne sur les vrais motifs de l'exil du poète de *L'Art d'aimer.*'

5. Alessandro Barchiesi, *Il poeta e la principe: Ovidio e il discorso augusteo* (Bari: Laterza, 1994).

6. Eratosthenes *Frag.* 1.A.16, cited by Strabo *Geography* 1.2.15. English translation by Horace Leonard Jones for the Loeb Classical Library (London: Heinemann and Cambridge, Ma.: Harvard University Press, 1969), 1: 87.

7. *The Authoress of the Odyssey, Where and When She Wrote, Who She Was, the Use She Made of the 'Iliad', & How the Poem Grew Under Her Hands* (London: Macmillan, 1897); Maurizio Bettini, 'Il genere dei libri' in *Maschile/ femminile: Genere e ruoli nelle culture antiche*, ed. Maurizio Bettini (Bari: Laterza, 1993), 3-25.

8. In his 'Remarks' on the *Discourse of Free-Thinking*, published by Anthony Collins in 1713, also in *Theological Writings*, vol. 3 of *The Works of Richard Bentley*, ed. Alexander Dyce (London, 1838; repr. New York: AMS Press, 1966), 304. Cf. R.C. Jebb, *Bentley* (London: Macmillan, 1898), 147. It is difficult to avoid the impression that Robert Graves had precisely these words of Bentley's in mind when he wrote the conclusion to his novel, *Homer's Daughter*. Nausicaa, the fictitious author of the *Odyssey*, actually says: 'The *Iliad*, which I admire, is devised by a man for men; this epic, the *Odyssey*, will be devised by a woman for women.' Bentley was highly regarded; his judgement was cited by Butler, *The Authoress*, as early as p. 4 (for Graves' novel, see n. 13 below).

9. Ptolemaeus Chennos, *Kainê historia*, Photius, *Bibliotheca* 190 (151b); I owe this quotation to my friend Luigi Spina, 'doctissimus neapolites'. Anton Chatzís, *Der Philosoph und Grammatiker Ptolemaios Chennos: Leben, Schriftstellerei, und Fragmente (mit Ausschluß der Aristotelesbiographie)*, Erster Teil, *Einleitung und Text*, Studien zur

Geschichte und Kultur des Altertums, Band 7, Heft 2 (Paderborn, 1914; repr. New York and London: Johnson Reprint, 1967), 36.

10. Where the story is also found: *Eustathii Comentarii ad Homeri Odysseam* (Leipzig, 1825; repr. Hildesheim: Georg Olms, 1960), 1: 2. Eustathius (d. *c.* 1194) was a Greek scholar and commentator, born and educated in Constantinople where he taught rhetoric in the Patriarchal School.

11. Philip Henderson, *Samuel Butler: The Incarnate Bachelor* (New York: Barnes & Noble, 1967), 231. Henderson's biography provides plenty of information about Butler's Homeric theories, from his first lecture on the subject (received with mordant scepticism by Jane Harrison) to his triumphs in Trapani and in Italy in general.

12. Butler, *The Authoress*, 207. Nausicaa, the mythological daughter of Alcinous, fed and clothed the shipwrecked Odysseus and showed him the way to the palace in Phaeacia.

13. Robert Graves, *Homer's Daughter* (Garden City, N.Y.: Doubleday, 1955), esp. 190-1.

14. Lewis Greville Pocock, *The Sicilian Origin of the Odyssey* (Wellington: New Zealand University Press, 1957). By the same author, *Reality and Allegory in the Odyssey* (Amsterdam: Hakkert, 1959).

15. Paris: Augustin, 1992.

16. Palermo: Flaccovio, 1967.

17. *Il Giornale di Sicilia*, 6 March 1968. I owe the preceding information on the theories of Homeric geography in Sicily to Gennaro D'Ippolito, and in particular to his contribution 'Malta nell'Odissea? Considerazioni sulla geografia omerica', *Kokalos* 22-3 (1976-77), 400ff.

18. *Der Weg des Odysseus: Tunis, Malta, Italien in den Augen Homers* (Tübingen: E. Wasmuth, 1968); *Die wirkliche Reise des Odysseus* (Munich: Langen Müller, 1983). Cf. Gioachino Chiarini, *Odisseo: Il labirinto marino* (Rome: Kepos, 1991), 49ff. Friedrich August Wolf (1759-1824), a German classical scholar who is often considered the founder of modern philology, discussed the question of the authorship of the Homeric poems.

19. *Odyssey* 9.292. See Chiarini, *Odisseo*.

20. Cf. Chiarini, *Odisseo*, 56. I owe much information about these passionate investigators of goatskins, cobblers and stitches to my friendship with the author.

21. Iman Wilkens, *Where Troy Once Stood* (New York: St Martin's Press, 1990).

22. Ibid., photo facing p. 177.

23. Margharita Guarducci, 'La casa di Properzio ad Assisi', *Atti del Convegno internazionale di Studi Properziani, Roma-Assisi 1985* (Assisi, 1986), 137ff., which summarises and concludes other work by the author in this topic.

Notes

24. A lively description of the origins of this science is found in Giuseppe Pucci, *Il passato prossimo: La scienza dell'antichità alle origini della cultura moderna* (Rome: La Nuova Italia Scientifica, 1993).

25. Alberto Ronchey (1926-), an Italian professor of sociology and journalist, recently served in the national government as Minister for Culture and the Environment.

26. Umberto Eco, *I limiti dell'interpretazione* (Milan: Bompiani, 1991), English translation: *The Limits of Interpretation* (Bloomington: Indiana University Press, 1990), 193: 'Authentic means historically original. To prove that an object is original means considering it as a sign of its own origins.'

27. *La Reppublica*, 17 June 1993.

28. Martial *Epigrams* 11.48 and 50, 12.65.5; cf also Pliny the Younger *Letters* 3.7.

29. Silius Italicus *Punica* 12.390-414, esp. 12.394-6: *hispida tellus / miserunt Calabri; Rudiae genuere vetustae; / nunc Rudiae solo memorabile nomen alumno* ('[Ennius] came from the rugged land of Calabria, and he was a son of ancient Rudiae – Rudiae which now owes all her fame to this child of hers'). English translation by J.D. Duff for the Loeb Classical Library (London: Heinemann and Cambridge, Ma.: Harvard University Press, 1961), 2: 177.

30. The founding father, in turn, had his own ancestors. Giuseppe Pucci, 'I padri di Indiana Jones: Prolegomeni ad ogni archeologia futura che voglia presentarsi come mito', *Studi Urbinati* no. 64 (1991): 247ff.

31. The scholarly works, lyric poetry and political satire of Leopardi (1798-1837) rank him among the great Italian writers of his era.

32. Aristotle *Poetics* 8.3, 1451a. [tr. R.L.]

33. Abdullah Razi, *The Unknown 'Odyssey'* (Ankara: University Press, 1894).

34. *A Vindication of Abdullah Razi* (Montevideo: Publicaciones Tortilla, 1963).

35. Homer and Associates, *A Bedside Odyssey* (London: Olympia Press, 1966). I have drawn my account so far from the Preface to this short volume, together with the supporting, and obviously unreliable, bibliographical references.

36. Ibid., 13.

37. Demetrius *On Style* 3.189.

38. Sotades *Frag.* 4a, in *Collectanea Alexandrina: Reliquiae minores poetarum Graecorum aetatis Ptolemaicae 323-146 B.C.*, ed. John U. Powell (Oxford, 1925; repr. Chicago: Ares, 1981), 239.

39. Sotades *Frag.* 1 (Powell 238).

40. Benedetto Croce, 'Catullo: Carme LXXVI', in *Poesia antica e moderna: Interpretazioni* (Bari: Laterza, 1966), 66f. Croce (1866-1952) was an Italian historian, literary critic and philosopher of the Idealist school.

41. T.S. Eliot, 'What is a Classic' in *On Poetry and Poets* (London: Faber & Faber, 1957), 53ff.

42. 'Exposito Virgilianae continentiae secundum philosophos moralis', in *Fabii Fulgentii Planciadis Opera*, ed. Rudolf Helm (Leipzig, 1898; repr. Stuttgart: Teubner, 1970), 81ff.

43. Ibid., 84.

44. Frederick Ahl, *Sophocles 'Oedipus': Evidence and Self-Conviction* (Ithaca and London: Cornell University Press, 1991).

45. 'Expositio Virgilianae continentiae', 86.

46. Ibid., 103.

47. *Corriere della Sera*, 1 May 1993.

48. *Corriere della Sera*, 3 May 1993.

49. *Corriere della Sera*, 14 May 1993.

50. *Corriere della Sera*, 3 May 1993.

51. *La Reppublica*, 19 April 1994.

52. *Corriere della Sera*, 7 October 1993.

53. Maurizio Bettini, 'Una serata in casa di Jules Renard', Introduction to Jean-Pierre Vernant and Pierre Vidal-Naquet, *Mito e tragedia II* (Turin: Einaudi, 1991).

54. Hippolytus *Refutationes* 5.9.7 (*Refutatio omnium haeresium*, ed. Miroslav Marcovich, Patristische Texte und Studien, 25 (Berlin and New York: Walter de Gruyter, 1986), 166.

55. The Italian poet Lorenzo Da Ponte (Emmanuele Conegliano, 1749-1838) wrote the libretto for several of Mozart's operas, including *Don Giovanni* (1787).

56. Domenico Comparetti, *Virgilio nel medioevo*, ed. Giorgio Pasquali (Florence: La Nuova Italia, 1937), 1: 139.

57. Aulus Gellius *Noctes Atticae* 19.8.15, English translation by John C. Rolfe for the Loeb Classical Library (London: Heinemann and Cambridge, Ma.: Harvard University Press, 1927-8), 3: 377.

58. Ibid., 6.13.1-2 (Rolfe 2: 59-61).

59. Ibid., 16.10.15 (Rolfe 3: 171).

60. Ibid., 16.10.11 (Rolfe 3: 169).

61. Ibid., 16.10.13 (Rolfe 3: 171).

62. Sextus Pompeius Festus, *De verborum significatu quae supersunt cum Pauli epitome*, ed. Wallace M. Lindsay (Leipzig: Teubner, 1913), 49.14-15.

63. Jorge Luis Borges and Osvaldo Ferrari, *Dialogos* (Barcelona: Seix Barral, 1992), 83.

64. Eugenio Montale (1896-1981) was one of the greatest Italian poets of the twentieth century and winner of the Nobel Prize for literature in 1975. His wife Drusilla Tanzi, nicknamed 'Mosca' ('Fly'), died in 1963.

65. Montale, *Sulla poesia*, ed. Giorio Zampa (Milan: Mondadori, 1976), 606.

66. Montale, 'Variazioni', in *Corriere della Sera*, 27 March 1974. Zampa did not include this particular 'variazione' in the volume cited above.

67. Italo Calvino, *Perché leggere i classici* (Milan: Mondadori, 1991), 1ff.

68. A well known fact. See, e.g., F. Scott Fitzgerald, *The Great Gatsby*, Introduction by Charles Scribner III (New York: Collier Books, 1980), xiii.

69. Pier Paolo Pasolini, *Petrolio* (Turin: Einaudi, 1992), 4.

70. Tabucchi (1943-), an Italian professor, novelist and poet, achieved international fame with his novel *Sostiene Pereira* (1994).

71. The English translation of Montale's verse about Mosca is that of Glauco Cambon, *Eugenio Montale's Poetry*: *A Dream in Reason's Presence* (Princeton, N.J.: Princeton University Press, 1982), 212.

72. Catullus *Carmina* 95, English translation by F.W. Cornish for the Loeb Classical Library (London: Heinemann and New York: G.P. Putnam's Sons, 1913), 167.

73. In a similar vein, Horace recommends that you wait 'nine years' before publishing any composition; see *Ars poetica* 388-90.

74. Giorgio Baffo (1694-1768) was a celebrated Venetian poet and libertine.

75. Eugenio Montale, 'I nuovi iconografi', in *Diario del '72*: *L'opera in versi* (Turin: Einaudi, 1980), 483. [Tr. R.L.]

7. The Classics in an Age of Indiscretion

1. It was published, for instance, in *Sophocle I*, ed. Paul Masqueray (Paris: Les Belles Lettres, 1929), also in *Sophocle*, vol. 1, *Les Trachiniennes – Antigone*, ed. Alphonse Dain, tr. Paul Mazon, corr. Jean Irigoin (Paris: Les Belles Lettres, 1981), lxix-lxxii.

2. Athenaeus *Deipnosophists* 13.81.603E-604D.

3. On 'gossip' in Suetonius, see Gianni Guastella, 'Suetonio e Caligola: La biografia senza la storia', in *G. Suetonio Tranquillo*: *La vita di Caligola* (Rome: La Nuova Italia Scientifica, 1992).

4. It is generally thought that Suetonius' *De poetis* is the source for the *Vita Vergilii* that has come down to us as the work of the grammarian Aelius Donatus: see Augusto Rostagni, *Suetonio 'De poetis' e biografi minori* (Turin: Loescher, 1964), 68-107. In the course of transmission, the original biographical core has been considerably amplified by further information and revision. Consequently, not all the Vergilian 'indiscretions' I will mention can be ascribed to Suetonius. The *Vitae Vergilianae* are cited from the edition of Jacob Brummer (Leipzig: Teubner, 1912).

5. *Vita Donatiana*, ed. Rostagni, 29-35.

6. Ibid., 50.

7. *Vitae Vergilianae*, ed. Brummer, 32.

8. *Vita Donatiana*, ed. Rostagni, 95-9.

9. Corydon is a character in Vergil's Second *Eclogue* who laments that his love for the boy Alexis is not reciprocated.

10. Macrobius *Saturnalia* 6.1.1-6.6.19, English translation by Percival Vaughan Davies, *Records of Civilisation: Sources and Studies*, 79 (New York and London: Columbia University Press, 1969), 385-6.

11. *Vitae Vergilianae*, ed. Brummer, 31.

12. *Vita Donatiana*, ed. Rostagni, 180.

13. Macrobius *Saturnalia* 6.1.2, 6.1.5.

14. *Vita Donatiana*, ed. Rostagni, 190.

15. Gaius Cornelius Gallus (*c.* 69-26 BC) was a Roman poet, general, and at one time a close political associate of Augustus. Vergil made him the protagonist of his Tenth Eclogue.

Epilogue

1. *Stromateis* 1.1.1-1.14.4. [tr. R.L.]

2. Ibid., 1.2.2. Clement here uses a well-known Greek proverb, whose meaning roughly corresponds to our 'pearls before swine'.

3. Ibid., 1.5.1.

4. Ibid., 1.7.1, tr. John Ferguson, *Stromateis, Books One to Three*, The Fathers of the Church, 85 (Washington, D.C.: Catholic University of America Press, 1991), 27.

5. Ibid., 1.9.1, tr. Ferguson, 28.

6. Ibid., 1.9.2, tr. Ferguson, 28-9.

7. Ibid., 1.14.2, tr. Ferguson, 32.

8. Ibid., 1.14.3-4, tr. Ferguson, 32-3.

9. Plato *Letters* 7.342Aff., English translation by R.G. Bury for the Loeb Classical Library (London: Heinemann and New York: G.P. Putnam's Sons, 1929), 533ff. We are dealing with a text so thoroughly studied by scholars that it would be out of place, in this context, to attempt to cite all the relevant bibliography. Among the most recent studies, see Giovanni Cerri, *Platone sociologo della comunicazione* (Milan: Il Saggiatore, 1991), 90ff. On p. 90 n. 20 you will find the essential references regarding the tortuous problem of the authenticity of the letter (today considered authentic by the majority of scholars).

10. Plato *Letters* 7.344Bff., tr. Bury, 539-41. The citation combines two passages from the *Iliad*, 7.360 and 12.234.

11. Cerri, *Platone sociologo*, 83ff.

12. *Phaedrus* 275Dff., English translation by Harold North Fowler for the Loeb Classical Library (London: Heinemann and Cambridge, Ma.: Harvard University Press, 1971), 565-7.

13. The second letter of Plato is still considered spurious by scholars: Giorgio Pasquali, *Le lettere di Platone* (Florence: Le Monnier, 1938), 173; Cerri, *Platone sociologo*.

Notes

14. Plato *Letters* 2.314Aff., tr. Bury, 415.

15. Plautus *Mostellaria* 473.

16. Homer *Iliad* 6.168-70, English translation by Richmond Lattimore (Chicago: University of Chicago Press, 1951), 157.

17. Claude Lévi-Strauss, *Tristes Tropiques* (Paris: Plon, 1955).

18. Maurizio Bettini, *Il ritratto dell'amante* (Turin: Einaudi, 1992), 136-7, English translation by Laura Gibbs, *The Portrait of the Lover* (Berkeley, Los Angeles and London: University of California Press, 1998).

19. Fridericus Boehm, *De symbolis Pythagoreis* (Berlin: M. Driesner, 1905).

Index

Index